The Sea is so Great

A small boat voyage in the Pacific Ocean

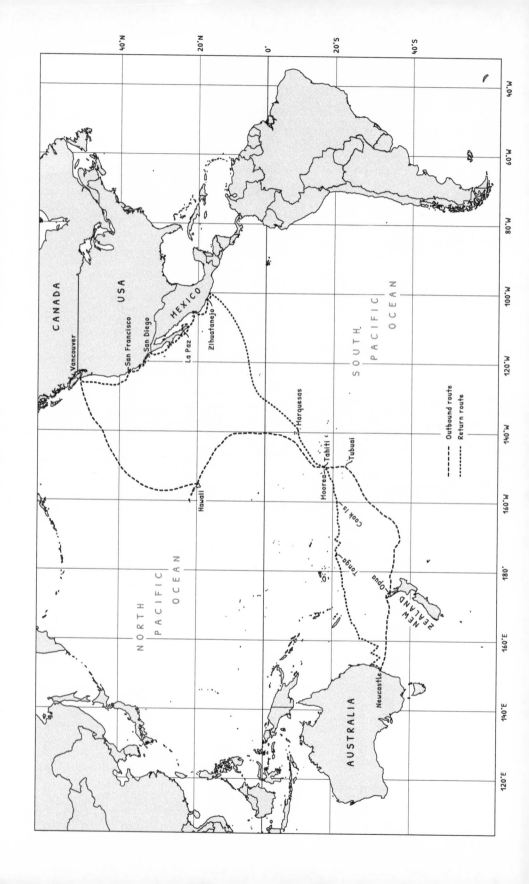

THE SEA IS
SO GREAT

A small boat voyage
in the Pacific Ocean

Alan Nebauer

IMPERATOR
PUBLISHING

Imperator Publishing
35 Burnham Avenue, Bognor Regis, PO21 2JU, England
www.imperator.pub

The author appreciates the good advice and assistance he received from his
editor, Yani Silvana.

A catalogue record for this book is available from the British Library.

First edition published 2019

ISBN 978-1-912784-02-8

For Cindy, Annie, and Vance

Contents

I

The Best Laid Plans

I REMEMBER AS AN EIGHT-YEAR-OLD telling my grandmother that I was going to sail around the world. She laughed – a full-on belly laugh! She wasn't being unkind – I was just a kid living with my parents and five siblings in a small Hunter Valley town more than two hours from the coast.

However, I never lost the driving ambition to sail and cruise aboard my own yacht: my ultimate goal was to make a solo circumnavigation of the world. I am not sure what motivates someone so young to have such a specific goal, but for me it was very clear. The first solo circumnavigations had just been made – Knox-Johnston and Chichester most recently – so perhaps a random news report grabbed my attention and stuck. My family were not seafarers.

Fortunately Mum and Dad always encouraged us to do the things we wanted to do. Each weekend they would take me and my 8-foot dinghy to the local sailing club, which was set up on an artificial lake that provided cooling water for a power station. I started as an 11-year-old, moving through a succession of used dinghies that we bought and fixed up. My brothers would crew for me, sometimes reluctantly, but we had fun. Once we enjoyed a fast reach across the lake so much that we abandoned the club race to turn around to repeat that exhilarating leg!

At age 16 I managed to talk my way onto an offshore boat – *Penando*, an old wooden Sparkman and Stephens 40-foot sloop which was preparing for the 1979 Sydney to Hobart race. The boat was based in Sydney and I would catch a ride down each weekend with one of the network of trucks that delivered newspapers around the state – maniacal drivers on deadlines, so it was always a quick trip. The Kiwi owner of *Penando*, Jack Allen, missed the timing for his entry paperwork for the race, but he sailed with the fleet anyway. We took it as a training run, as we were entered in the 1980 Hobart to Auckland race shortly after new year. I was delighted to be included with the five other crew. Being the youngest on board, I was the brunt of some humour, but I knew I had a lot to discover and felt that I was on the cusp of something big. The trip was a great opportunity for me to gain experience I would need to sail my own ocean-going yacht – fundamental things like watch keeping and working together for sail changes and manoeuvres; and realising that the demands of the boat dictated schedules of life on board and could never be ignored. I ended up getting more than I bargained for!

A severe tropical storm developed over northern Australia, entering the Tasman Sea as a fully formed cyclone (Cyclone Paul, 80+ knots), wreaking havoc among the fleet midway to New Zealand. Most of the boats were damaged in the extreme conditions, and the high-profile kiwi yacht *Smackwater Jack* was lost along with all four crew members.

At the height of the storm we endured 30 hours of sustained winds in excess of 70 knots and 50-foot-plus tumbling great seas. Several times our boat was picked up and smashed down by mountainous seas, putting the mast underwater – and at one point dislodging the engine. As a result, we could no longer charge the batteries and were without radio communications. Two other boats were also out of radio contact for several days during and after the storm, causing concern for authorities and families ashore.

The weather had settled as we neared Cape Reinga a few days later, and we crossed paths with another racing yacht, *Quicksilver*. We were able to check in with them, speaking across the water as the boats sailed for a while side by side in the

Crew of Penando *in Auckland after the 1980 Hobart–Auckland Race*

flat seas. They were able to report us safe to the race committee. We hoped that *Smackwater Jack* was just having radio problems, as we had, but sadly this was not the case. Nothing was ever heard from them again.

New Zealand yachtsman Sir Peter Blake, who was caught out in the same storm, described it as the most severe weather he had ever encountered in an interview published in Lin and Larry Pardey's *Storm Tactics*:

> While delivering the 76-foot maxi Condor *back to New Zealand after the [1979] Sydney-Hobart Race, two New Zealand boats were caught in a tropical cyclone that turned south to collide with an intense low-pressure system in the Tasman Sea. The New Zealand and Australian meteorological services later confirmed this as a double cyclone. Ships in the area reported wind speeds exceeding 100 knots, with gusts of 120 and seas of corresponding severity. "When things began going bad, I made the decision to turn into the wind and heave to. It is the first and only time I came close to a crew mutiny. In fact, that was the hardest part of the whole affair, heaving to in spite of all the crew pressure to run before the storm." The second hardest part, according to Peter, was listening to the Maydays coming from the crew on another New Zealand-bound yacht. "Condor lay really well," Peter stated. At the height of the storm, which lasted for about 35 hours, the motion was far from easy, and Peter did wonder what he would do if the trysail failed. Sadly, the second of three New Zealand yachts,* Smack Water Jack *and her crew – which at the beginning of the storm had been within 40 miles of* Condor *– was lost while running in front of the cyclone. The conjecture is that her course led directly into the second low-pressure system.*
> — Storm Tactics, Lin & Larry Pardey

Sometimes, ignorance is bliss. During the storm I probably wasn't aware how serious the situation was, as we passed the point of control and huge breaking seas raged around us. It did set a high threshold for me – I was thinking wet and miserable must be par for the course, and that good days were a bonus. It was almost fifteen years before I saw similar conditions again. I gained an early understanding and respect for how impartial the sea is and the importance of planning and good seamanship. Still, a successful outcome was not always entirely up to us.

Over the next few years, crewing on different boats, I made several other cruises and deliveries to and from New Zealand, once even making it as far as Tahiti in idyllic French Polynesia.

When I was 19 I flew to Europe, spending a summer in Scotland as mate on a former Whitbread Round the World Race boat at an adventure school. The owner of the operation was former SAS Captain John Ridgeway, one of the pioneering skippers in The Golden Globe – the first non-stop, single-handed yacht race around the world, in 1968. Since then he had undertaken a major adventure or expedition each year, often at sea, and had built a name for himself as a tough, hard-driving leader. He had provided opportunities for lots of young people to gain life experience, and inspired them to pursue their own endeavours.

As instructors, we took small groups of businessmen on sailing expeditions on the Scottish west coast and rugged Atlantic Islands of St Kilda and the Outer Hebrides. The sailing was tough and challenging in the high latitudes, with changeable, often harsh weather. I was teamed up with the young skipper Andy Briggs. He was a very serious character, though friendly, and I enjoyed working with him. He was someone I could relate to and I admired his calm and methodical manner.

I was unsettled back at the adventure school, and found the larger group dynamic and cluster of instructors and course members harder to relate to than the smaller groups out at sea, where roles were more clearly defined. I respected the crotchety Ridgeway, and I always felt he liked me, but we did clash occasionally. He wasn't used to the outspoken Aussie nature, and once or twice it was, "My office, Mr Nebauer!" and I would march up the hill to the croft overlooking Loch Laxford for a 'chat'.

After returning home from Scotland, between sailing trips I would work at various jobs to save for the next opportunity to sail away. It was rare to be paid for crewing offshore; rather, you had to pay for the privilege. Crew would share expenses, provide labour, and contribute to maintenance costs to help look after the boat. But I wasn't complaining. To find the money for this lifestyle I did a stint as a baker early on and worked in boatyards when I could. After a while I found high-paying jobs on large concrete construction projects: I would spend a year or so working hard, followed by periods of several months sailing and travelling, before running out of money and starting the process again.

Each escapade taught me more about sailing, seamanship, and commitment, not to mention living with an assortment of people from varying backgrounds and countries. I have always been pretty conservative and found it a bit challenging, for example, sleeping on the deck of an American 37-footer in Auckland between boats and trying to find a way to politely refuse the pot-smoking owners' insistent offers to share their stash without offending them; they already thought it weird that I was an Aussie and didn't drink beer.

Sailing with and for other people was a great way to learn, but it was a short-term strategy, a starting point, a logical stepping stone that would help me gain confidence and experience: I was determined to eventually build my own yacht and sail away.

In early 1985, just a few months after I had launched my first small yacht – a 20-foot design that I had fitted out from a partially-built steel hull and deck in the back yard of a neighbour – I was offered a job with a survey field party on a gas pipeline project in the Northern Territory.

We spent almost 18 months in the central Australian desert, laying the route for one of the longest pipelines ever built in the country. At first I didn't enjoy the desert; it was hot, incredibly dry and dusty, and far removed from the sea and sailing – but the money was good and the work was interesting. After a while I came to love the desert – the flat, rugged landscape became familiar to me; it was beautiful. The vast, sweeping vista and huge sky reminded me of being at sea, far away from everything. The isolation was a tonic.

However, even in the dead centre of the Australian continent, preparation continued for ocean sailing. Brian Dewing, the lead project surveyor, was a friend. He had been the navigator on that first crossing of the Tasman Sea, five years earlier on the old wooden sloop *Penando*, when we had wondered if we might not make it out the other side of a cyclone.

At school maths had never been my strong point, but Brian pushed me, posing celestial navigation problems for me to solve. He related it all back to the terrestrial project we were involved with, where we ran azimuths calculated from daylight-viewable stars (viewed with high-magnification instruments) to keep the 1500-kilometre survey traverse aligned. I found it a real challenge, but gradually the slightly out-of-context ocean navigation principles became clearer in the haze of the desert heat.

We worked in a four-man field party, thirty days on, seven off, on rotation. During the breaks I would fly home, and live on my boat. Once, during a two-month wet season shut-down, I sailed with a novice owner, on his recently acquired ketch, from Sydney to New Zealand. While there I delivered another yacht up the Kiwi coast with some young Canadian backpackers, before returning to the pipeline project in central Australia. That voyage, and the time spent away, confirmed for me that I was ready for a slightly larger yacht, more suited to the long-distance ocean sailing I craved.

Originally, I thought I would like a Vertue 25 or a Folkboat – both well-known international classes and respected as good small cruising boats. I had also come to admire a yacht built on the Australian east coast that offered similar design attributes. It was more affordable and had a good reputation as being seaworthy and tough – which was reinforced by articles I had read by a Sydney couple, Ian and Jan Mitchell, who had made a world circumnavigation aboard their 'Top Hat' yacht *Caprice*. So, after a test sail on a factory demo boat and some consideration, I felt comfortable making a decision.

Calling the boat builders from a hotel phone almost 3000 kilometres away in Alice Springs, I placed the order for the hull and deck shell of a fibreglass, John Illingworth–designed, 25-foot Top Hat. On my return to the coast, we trucked the mouldings closer to home and I proceeded to fit out the new boat during my regular weeks off. I would sleep in my car parked next to the boat, at the marina yard on Lake Macquarie, near Newcastle. After about six months of part-time and some full-time work, I launched the boat in November 1986.

Deus Regit II was complete, but very basic. The pipeline project I had been

Early days of the fitout of Deus Regit II *at Marmong Cove Marina, near Newcastle*

working on in central Australia had been completed a couple of months ahead of schedule, and my budget was reduced accordingly. I had not been able to get everything on my wish list and lacked some equipment: I had only a mechanical Sumlog to record speed and distance, and no depth or wind instruments. But with the basics covered and a small but substantial yacht under my feet it felt like my childhood goal of sailing around the world was in the process of becoming a reality. I prepared for an open-ended cruise across the Pacific.

The plan was to sail solo from Australia across the Pacific to Canada via New Zealand, French Polynesia, and Hawaii, setting out in mid-February on what would be my fourth Tasman crossing. But there is a saying about 'best laid plans', and I was to learn that timing and wonderful opportunities can surprise us, so it's probably a good idea to be flexible.

In the weeks prior to my scheduled departure I had met a girl, Cressinda Smith – or Cindy. We were briefly introduced after a church service, and I was instantly taken by her smile and natural beauty; her casual Aussie-girl style was complemented by a nice tan and a ready wit. A week later we made a deeper connection when, seated side by side ('set up') at a mutual friend's wedding, we spent the day together. We had lots to talk about and found that we shared similar ideals. Also, Cindy was ready for adventure: she was about to embark on a trip to the

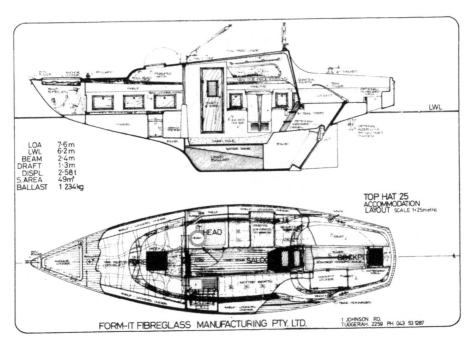

Layout of the Top Hat 25

States with her sister and she was interested to hear of my imminent plans to head off cruising.

Cindy and her sister Vanessa offered to help with shopping for provisions for my trip, and by way of thanks I invited them both to dinner on board. It was a memorable night: Vess seemed intent on ensuring that her sister wasn't being lured in by some sailor who might have a girl in every port. In addition, she almost set fire to the boat! I had not yet wired up a light in the head compartment and so she placed a candle on the shelf under the side deck. It wasn't long before the paint started to blister... and it was a bit chaotic for her in that compact, unfamiliar space for a moment or two! Fortunately she beat out the small flames with a towel and there was no permanent damage, either to the boat or to Vess.

I am not sure if it was my cooking or the moonlight sail that impressed Cindy, but shortly after, we decided to get married and sail together to Canada. I ended up delaying my departure – and at the same time, with no regrets, unconsciously shelving the 'solo' part of my sailing ambitions – and Cindy never flew to the USA.

It all sounded pretty simple to me, but it turned out that wedding arrangements and convincing family of the virtues of a long ocean honeymoon take time. Having made a shakedown passage to Coffs Harbour, I shelved further plans to sail to New Zealand before the wedding, as my proposal was causing tension in Cindy's family. Her dad was threatening to call it off! I returned, to give them an opportunity get to know me and so that I could help out with the impromptu wedding plans. Eventually, at the end of April 1987, about ten weeks after we first met, we sailed from our home port of Newcastle.

Friends and family had gathered on the old police dock on the foreshore to see us off. Cindy's elderly grandmother, desperate to see inside the boat, slipped as she struggled down the rickety steel ladder; fortunately I caught her just as her feet hit the water! She scrambled over the side with some help, only slightly worse for wear. Apart from this, we got away without incident. We had been married nine days; Cindy was 21 and I had just turned 24.

II

Across the Tasman Sea to New Zealand

O UR FIRST LEG would take us 1000 miles across the Tasman Sea to North Cape, New Zealand, followed by a coastal hop a further 100 miles south to Opua in the Bay of Islands. The Tasman has a fierce reputation as a rugged place for sailors; the pilot books predict that one should expect at least one gale on a crossing. We expected to be at sea about ten to fourteen days.

After leaving Newcastle in a moderate northerly breeze, a gale set in on the second day. Keeping with Tasman tradition the winds remained fresh for the rest of that first week, and we made reasonable progress. Then the wind and our boat speed tapered off to zero, leaving us drifting towards our landfall off Cape Reinga, at the northern tip of New Zealand. For Cindy this was a robust introduction to sailing, let alone passage making. She'd had no experience before we left, apart from a few quiet day sails, and had no idea what to expect at sea or even if she would like it. Part of Cindy's preparation for life on a boat consisted of a shopping day with Vess when she bought five bikinis! I thought this was a very nice idea, but I did suggest we head down to the local chandlery to buy a set of Line 7 foul-weather gear for her, just in case it wasn't all sunshine.

It was an exciting time for us: it was the first time Cindy had left Australia, and we had plenty of adjustments to make, suddenly living together 24/7 in an unusual environment and perhaps at closer quarters than most newly-weds.

The rough seas, ceaseless motion and the splashing sounds of a small boat scooting through the waves were all new for Cindy. When it was dark she was never sure whether we were sinking or if it was merely one more wave crashing over us. Coming below one evening I found her anxiously crawling around, hands feeling forward in the forepeak, checking that the bow had not been stove in as we bashed into yet another solid lump of a wave.

Taking well-intended advice from various people on the best remedy for sea-

An early sail with Cindy aboard Deus Regit II

sickness, and in an effort to keep this unfamiliar malady at bay, Cindy tried several methods in turn. The inadvertent overlap resulted in an overdose of a mixture of scopolamine and Stugeron, which caused lethargy and even delirium and made it hard for her body to adapt. The preventative had become far worse than any case of 'mal de mer'. Realising her mistake, Cindy went cold turkey. After a week or so on a diet of grated apples she started to emerge from a drug-induced haze, vowing off seasick pills forever.

Back then, expectations and requirements for what gear to take on board were quite different to the equipment and technology available today. Boats were simpler and systems basic, not having changed much in the preceding few decades during which people had been enjoying ocean sailing. We had no satnav or GPS, no dinghy (ours had been stolen the week prior to leaving), no VHF radio, and no liferaft. We had only one 12-volt battery and a small solar panel that was barely able to keep up with the demand of our short-wave radio receiver, interior lighting, and occasional use of navigation lights when in the vicinity of a coast or shipping traffic.

My focus before setting out had been to make my simple boat as seaworthy as possible. I had had a spray dodger made, and this contributed dramatically to onboard comfort by providing shelter from the sometimes relentless spray, helping keep us and, importantly, the interior dry. In addition to slightly oversized standing rigging, I had set up an inner forestay for a small staysail that could be slab reefed to storm jib size. This was backed up with simple running backstays that could be set up to help support the mast in heavy weather.

One concession towards technology that I did make was to install an Autohelm 1000 (now Raymarine) autopilot. We used this little gem on departure, but after the first few days in rough, overcast weather, it was apparent that our electrics and small solar panel were not up to the task. It only really worked when we were motoring and the outboard motor was producing a few amps of current, taking care of the pilot's draw from the battery.

Unable to depend on the pilot, we were forced to improvise and get the boat to self-steer with a sheet-to-tiller method. This proved surprisingly effective and worked for all points of sail, removing the need for us to constantly hand steer. We set up the back-winded staysail with the sheets led to the windward side of the tiller. The pull from this small sail was opposed by a strong bungy elastic on the opposite side of the tiller, developing an equilibrium as the boat would first head up, then bear away, in response to the different wind and conditions. We sailed a slightly weaving pattern to maintain an average course. It was a useful system, though actually quite inefficient when compared to a well-designed mechanical

Deus Regit II *sailing herself on a nice day. You can see the back-winded staysail working in the gentle breeze to allow her to self-steer.*

windvane self-steering gear or to a reliable autopilot. Often, to preserve the fine balance, the sails might be underpowered or not trimmed to the optimum as they would be when hand steering.

Overall it was an acceptable compromise, and we were delighted with the results. There was something special and pure about being able to sail 24/7 by balancing the sails only, enabling steady progress. We were able to eat, sleep, and navigate – in effect, to live – free from the need to hand steer continually. I had previously read of other boats making long voyages with the sheet-to-tiller method but hadn't tried it myself on *Deus Regit II* until I was forced to get creative mid-Tasman, so we were both pleasantly surprised when I set it up and it was working from the get-go. Of course, we refined the process and improved our technique as we went along, but it was reassuring at that early stage to see that the boat would self-steer easily due to her nicely balanced hull and sail plan. Cindy thought I was very clever and I wasn't about to deny the kudos.

After a stormy, bumpy crossing of the Tasman, the wind dropped off and for the last part we drifted on glassy seas, taking four days to make good the last 180 nautical miles. After 15 days, we finally arrived in the Bay of Islands well after mid-night. We only carried about 20 litres of petrol for the outboard, and had exhausted our supply a couple of days earlier when the wind dropped off while we were work-ing around a headland against a current. I had failed to keep a reserve, optimisti-cally assuming that the wind would shortly return. But it didn't!

Tired and a little ragged, we worked the last few miles up the river in the dead of night towards Opua, our official port of arrival. At some point, passing small islands and with the lights of villages coming into view, we broke through the fatigue and, with the excitement of our hard-won progress, we started to appreci-ate the challenging conditions. Thankfully, we squeezed all we could – sometimes with barely any steerage way – from the patchy zephyrs of shifting air.

At about 3:30 a.m. we ghosted gently alongside, tying to a convenient floating dock belonging to a local charter company, and promptly went to sleep.

III

Bay of Islands: Drug Runners and Body Bags

EARLY THE NEXT MORNING we were startled awake by a friendly cry of "Ahoy, *Deus Regit!*" It was Susan Hiscock, an old friend, who was rowing past in her dinghy and had noticed us tied to the wharf. I had come to know Susan several years before, when I met her and her husband, Eric, aboard their yacht *Wanderer IV*. The Hiscocks were an English couple famous in the sailing world, having been one of the first husband and wife teams to circumnavigate the world, in the early 1950s. With a later voyage they became the first couple to do so twice. Eric went on to write at least six books on the subject of cruising and voyaging under sail.

The Hiscocks had lived aboard full-time and eventually sailed more than three times around the world in over four decades of sailing together. Eric had died less than a year previously, and Susan – at that time well into her seventies – was living alone aboard the new and smaller 40-foot *Wanderer V*, which they had had built only a few years earlier.

It was a nice welcome to be greeted so enthusiastically by an old friend, and Susan made some polite comments about our capable-looking boat – though she seemed rather more pleased to meet Cindy, and to find that I was no longer sailing alone! We made plans to catch up later in the day. First, we had to complete arrival formalities by checking in with customs and immigration and passing the strict quarantine clearance.

I was taken aback by the agent's response when I phoned the customs office in Whangarei, announcing our arrival in Opua. When I told him my name and the boat's name he paused briefly, before declaring "You were crew last year on *Troubadour*, weren't you?" I confirmed that this was correct and tentatively asked why he was so quick to make the connection. "No worries," he said, "I'll tell you when I get there."

Before the customs officer arrived we went to collect our mail, which had been directed care of the Opua post office. The staff, Margaret and Helen, knew me from previous visits as a teenager and had noticed mail arriving addressed to me (based on my earlier ETA) and then to Cindy, so made the assumption we had married. They had been expectantly awaiting our arrival and we received a very warm welcome indeed, along with some nice mail from home.

Back on board, waiting for the customs officer, I was a little nervous. My experience with the boat the customs officer recalled so easily had been a bit weird. The owner, a rather refined businessman, and his leather-clad, outlaw-bikie-type crew had made an odd couple. Neither had sailed offshore before, but they had big plans to sail via New Zealand directly to Puerto Montt in Chile. Casting off in Sydney, the owner kissed his ex-wife goodbye as if he was going to the office. I was along as an experienced hand in response to a newspaper 'crew wanted' ad, and I had left the boat after the Tasman crossing as planned.

Back in Australia, a couple of months later I had received a call from the Australian Federal Police (AFP) and was interviewed extensively about the trip. They asked questions about the boat and specifically about the personality of the others on board; whether I recalled conversations or things the crew may have discussed, or whether I had any insight into how the crew interacted. While I was obliged to share my thoughts with the AFP, they could not tell me anything about an ongoing investigation. The full story had always remained a mystery to me.

When New Zealand customs finally arrived, over coffee the friendly officer filled us in on how the owner of *Troubadour* had been the subject of a joint Australian and New Zealand drug investigation. They had collaborated with international authorities to track the movements and whereabouts of the boat and her crew up until she was boarded on arrival in Australia many months later. The AFP were disappointed when no contraband was found. They still felt that they had been on the right track, and the investigation continued. I was amazed at how much specific information the authorities were able to gather and that even my name still rang bells. The agent stamped us in without any fuss and assured me that my name didn't have a black mark on it in the system by association. I guess it pays to be a nerd.

We spent a few weeks in Opua, in the beautiful Bay of Islands – a convenient stop on our route, and a place with strong connections for me from my travels as a teenager. We were on a tight budget, so I found some work at Deemings boat yard

– where I'd also worked on previous trips – to keep us going until we left, in early June, for Tahiti. The owners of the boat yard, Dick and Pat McIlvride, allowed us to use one of their moorings for free, calling it a wedding gift.

By now it was winter, and it would be getting colder on our southern route across the Pacific. We were due in Canada for a deadline mid-September, and we also wanted to beat the onset of the potentially severe autumn gales in the North Pacific. These concerns dictated what was to be a pretty rigorous schedule.

Some of the women on other cruising boats in port at the time were fascinated by Cindy and by the fact that we were newlyweds. They wondered how Cindy had been able to make such a radical, life-changing decision to get married and head off on a small boat within only a few weeks of knowing me, and having barely sailed before. Their experience was the inverse of ours; they had been sailing 'part-time' with their husbands and children for years, but only now that their kids were adults were they able to embark on the long-dreamed-of cruising adventure. They took Cindy under their wing and may even have felt a little bit protective of her. They made time to show her cooking tips and recommended nutritious recipes that were easy to prepare at sea. This was especially helpful, as our limited galley had neither fridge nor oven. Everything had to be cooked on the basic two-burner alcohol stove, and we selected and stored provisions carefully to last as long as possible.

Closer to our departure date, a workmate from the boat yard, 'Barry the Pom', and his wife Lilly offered to drive us to Whangerai, where we shopped in the large supermarket. This devoured most of the money I had earned working at Deemings, but by the end of the day we were well stocked and as ready as we could be.

We had also got to know Nick Skeates, who was sailing on his self-designed and self-built *Wylo II*. He was a real character, always happy to share a meal or two and helpful with suggestions on seamanship and voyaging, sharing in particular his experience with sheet-to-tiller self-steering. Susan Hiscock suggested that I ask him to check my sextant, as my navigation had been a little dodgy on the crossing from Australia. Nick took a look and adjusted some instrument error. I hoped this would improve the accuracy of my sights.

Nearing our time to leave Opua, we were back on the main wharf to meet with customs officers who had driven up to clear us for departure. While I was below with customs, Cindy was chatting with a woman from another boat in the cockpit and I overheard the woman make a comment about a 'cute little boat' that was just arriving at the wharf flying a yellow quarantine flag, indicating that it had just arrived from overseas.

I looked out of our cabin window as the boat turned to come alongside, and was surprised to recognise my old small steel boat – the original *Deus Regit* that I had built over a period of 13 months at my parents' home. I had left the boat with a broker when I took delivery of the hull and deck of *Deus Regit II*, and was never informed that she had been sold. It was an amazing sight – two small boats that I had launched, docked together in a foreign country!

Russell Salmon, the young Englishman who had bought *Deus Regit* in Australia just days before his visa expired, had sailed 30 days single-handed from Sydney, stopping briefly at Lord Howe Island, part way across the Tasman Sea. I was gobsmacked and couldn't believe the timing of the reunion. We invited Russ to join us for lunch and enjoyed hearing stories of his exploits.

After finalising the checkout procedures, we returned to our mooring off Deemings, and I went back to my job as I still had some tasks left to finish. We had motored over to clear customs early, as there was the opportunity to split the fee charged for the officers to travel the 100 kilometres up from Whangerai to clear boats for departure with another departing yacht. However, as fees don't apply when you arrive, and Russell qualified for this 'arrival fee waiver', customs didn't charge any of us! At the time this was a real break for Cindy and me.

The original 20 ft Deus Regit *with her new owner, Russel Salmon*

The next day we said farewell to Susan on *Wanderer V* and also to Jerri, a young American we'd met while we were there. Jerri was sailing aboard *Spindrift* – the double-ended gaff ketch I had sailed to Tahiti, six years before, with her previous owner, George Budd. Jerri had inherited the boat from George, who had died that season in Fiji. I was disappointed not to be able to see my old mentor, but over dinner Jerri had regaled us with recent stories of his sailing adventures with George. The two had become like father and son, and Jerri was devastated when George passed away suddenly from a heart attack. Frustrated by the Fijian authorities' delay in releasing George's body, Jerri had convinced two young vacationing European nurses he had met to 'assist' with collecting George's body from the hospital for burial at sea! Wheeling the 'borrowed' gurney along the streets of Suva, they reached the boat without being caught. After securing the bagged remains on *Spindrift*'s foredeck, they hastily set sail.

Things became complicated when they met with squally weather and the two nurses, green with seasickness, demanded to be returned to shore. Jerri, feeling emotional, had lost his bearings and was unable to see landmarks in the murky tropical rain, which had become a deluge. Needless to say, the ceremony was short and sweet – the weighted George was heaved over the side somewhere off the reef south of Suva – and Jerri recovered his bearings and returned the nurses to shore, though much further along the coast than he'd anticipated.

Dropping the mooring at Deemings, Cindy and I sailed to an anchorage at Te Hui, closer to the entrance of the Bay of Islands, where we could pick up some fresh water from a spring – at that time Opua dock water was not suitable to take on board. Two local yachts met us there; *Shaydar*, with Eddie and Claire, was sailing north to Tonga, while we were heading east, to French Polynesia; their friends on *Holly* also came to see us off. We enjoyed the camaraderie over a weekend, visiting each other's yachts and discussing weather and future plans.

Our plan was to follow the classic route as advised in the British Admiralty's *Ocean Passages of the World* – an old-world book of instructions put together by sailing-ship captains over hundreds of years. Although an alternate route via Tonga, Samoa, and Hawaii would have made three shorter legs – better for Cindy and even for me – the winds are less reliable, making it more suited to a boat with a diesel engine to motor through the doldrums crossing the equator. In a larger, more modern yacht this would have been preferable, but we treated our little boat like a traditional ship and went with the wind as much as we could.

IV

South Pacific

THE SECOND LEG of our journey was to be non-stop from the Bay of Islands to Tahiti, a passage of more than 2800 miles. It would see us run down our easting between the latitudes of 34 and 35 degrees south. (We ended up sailing down near 37° S for a while, which was way too far south at that time of year in such a small boat!) We could count on the northern extremity of the westerly breezes tracking across the Southern Ocean to kick us along and to provide a steady, favourable breeze (in direction, at least) until we could lay the Island of Tahiti by sailing diagonally across the south-east trade winds, allowing us to head into the more benign tropical regions.

With our targeted average of 100 miles per day we only expected the trip to take about four weeks, but as anything could happen to affect this hypothetical average we would tell our parents and friends before we left not to expect to hear from us for about six to eight weeks. They had no idea of what it was like at sea and how we might be slowed by calms or heavy weather or even equipment failure. So with no way to communicate while sailing, we would give them an ETA with lots of padding. Hopefully they would get used to not hearing from us and, with no news being good news, they would not worry about us. My folks were in a better position than Cindy's mum and dad, as they had become used to me taking off and they understood that passage making is not an exact science. That said, I think there were many times when they wondered how we were doing, and if and when they might hear from us again.

Leaving New Zealand on the back of a cold front provided us with fresh westerly winds that soon shifted into the south-west, and this solid breeze kept us tracking at a steady pace. This is a reliable strategy and stems from the old days when ships could not sail to windward very well and great detours would be made to keep the winds on a favourable quarter. These same favourable winds set a pattern that would keep us sailing to plan; the only hang-up with this route on a small boat is that you are out on the sea for a long time and the weather can be pretty boisterous. We had no real 'ultimate storm', but we sailed for many days in gale-force conditions and big, lumpy seas typical of those latitudes.

We had no GPS or satellite devices back then, though satnavs were available and common for commercial shipping. I had heard of a couple of larger yachts having navigation systems: the Hiscocks had installed one on *Wanderer V* as a test, though, treading cautiously, they still continued regular celestial checks. Electronic navigation devices were incredibly expensive and – a far cry from today – not many cruising people considered them necessary or even a seaworthy option. So for us navigation was basic and traditional – we relied on dead reckoning (DR) and celestial fixes obtained by sextant.

We sailed for many days in a combination of heavy air, rough seas, and consistently gloomy overcast weather that made it impossible to fix our position. After our initial departure point, off Cape Brett, we ran a DR plot for seven days based on our estimated speed, course, and distance for a given time, before we were finally able to obtain another position fix. It was not until the end of the second week that we achieved decent sun sights again, and then subsequently we had further sightings on days 18, 21, and 22 of the passage. All in all, due to a mix of bad weather and the instability of the cheap sextant I was using, not to mention some inexpe-

A young skipper, happy to be at sea   *Cindy on watch a few days into the passage*

rience on my part, we were able to calculate only eight celestial fixes during the month, with a distance spread of more than 2100 nautical miles.

We tried diligently each day, sometimes for hours, to shoot the sun accurately enough to work up a fix – or even a single line of position (LOP), which would have been something! I was fortunate in that Cindy, being new to this voyaging thing, wasn't really looking at the potential of weeks on the fringe of the Southern Ocean without an accurate position. So it was only me getting stressed... After all, we joked, eventually we would meet land again on the west coast of South America, only another 4000 miles to our east.

Cindy worked with me; she would wait patiently with a watch, pencil, and note pad, ready to record the time as I called "mark" and then read off the observed angle from the sextant. More often than not all the effort was to no avail due to the tough conditions, and I was unable to shoot the sun to a true horizon, making it impossible to work up an accurate sight.

To compound matters, a few days after leaving New Zealand our Sumlog, a small paddle wheel that was recording our speed and distance, failed; and from then on we had to rely on a guesstimate for measuring our daily distance run. Apart from how well you shoot and record the sun's angle, fixes made by crossing two or more position lines are only as accurate as your DR position, which is used for a start point and for the interval between sun sights, so it was easy for errors to creep in to our measured versus assumed progress.

The weather was marginal and the seas quite rough, but *Deus Regit II* was not causing us any anxiety as she chugged away relentlessly towards the mark. If progress seemed hesitant, it was because she was waiting for the skipper to provide some direction!

Days would run together and while the work of keeping the boat going, navigating, and taking care of routine matters on board never let up, we had time to read and enjoy getting to know each other. We talked about everything and shared anecdotes about our families and things we did as kids. It was cold down south and Cindy took to knitting, making us both warm jumpers along the way. She loved writing letters home to friends and family, and these would become journal-like epics, covering days and many pages before being signed off and placed in unsealed envelopes. We would add a little summary when we arrived in port, before sending them off en masse. We used to read aloud to each other at night; among others we enjoyed a series of books by the British author C S Lewis. It was a highlight of each day as we worked through the chapters – like having time out off the boat for a bit.

Eating was something we both looked forward to. Cindy took the lead here, as I have little interest in food – or at least, the preparation of it. She saw it as a challenge to create enticing meals from our onboard supplies. She sought inspiration in the couple of recipe books she had brought, adapting the complicated land-based kitchen instructions to our little nautical world with its simple galley, and coming up with great creations using our basic provisions. Every few days I would take a turn in the galley and present one of my special curries or rudimentary pasta dishes that didn't vary much but seemed to taste all right at the time. However, my offers to cook seemed to be taken up less often as time went on.

Water was always a consideration. Not that we ever ran out of it, but we were limited by what we could store. Early on, I was pretty strict about our water use and gamely suggested to Cindy that we only had enough to wash our hair once a week, in an effort to conserve the 130 litres we carried. After a quick rebuttal, I had to adapt my thinking. Cindy, aware of our limitations, made up her own mind as to how the water was spent and we developed efficient ways to use the small allowance we set ourselves. There is real satisfaction in being able to have refreshing 'shower' with a litre of water, and we no longer had limits on how often or how much, as rationing came naturally. Conservation is really about being sensible with what you have, so we never wasted a drop.

Most of the time the wind was blowing from the west. Occasionally it swung east to head us, but usually before long it would flick back round and gain strength as a new weather front rolled through, so we were able to maintain our course, gybing and adjusting the sails, reefing the mainsail as required and furling the genoa to suit, for good balance.

On several occasions we had winds above gale force, sustained in excess of 40 knots, creating heavy seas. In these uncomfortable conditions we initially opted to lie ahull – all sails furled and the boat drifting beam on to the wind and swell. This was a practice we quickly learnt not to rely on, nor to recommend. We found that well before conditions caused the seas to become large and unsettled enough to break, it was safest to set some sail and keep the boat moving, for control, or to heave to. Lying hove to, with small sails set aback slowing the boat almost to a stop, was a much safer option, offering a surprisingly stable orientation with the bow pointed about 50 degrees off the wind. The priority here was to not allow the boat to lie beam on to these big seas, which would place her in the position most vulnerable to breaking waves which can easily roll a yacht.

Sometimes, to keep the boat safe, we would hand steer for long stretches, and it was then that we regretted not having been able to afford to buy a proper wind vane self-steering system before we left. I was always impressed with Cindy's resilience, as she really had only been sailing for a few weeks. I would be on call for long periods, but we were becoming a team and she would always take her turn on the helm, even in these rough conditions, when our sail balance combination had passed its limit and we needed to help out in order to maintain progress and stay safe. Cindy would take over to give me a break at the tiller for an hour or two; and occasionally, sensing my fatigue, she would let me sleep longer to recover for the next watch.

On one of these early times, at the top end of our wind range, it had become difficult to balance the sails to stay on course and so we were lying ahull in heavy seas, with the boat turning sideways and drifting gently off to leeward. This had worked fine previously in moderate conditions, and it was reasonably comfortable; however, with the unstable breaking seas we ended up being knocked on our beam ends in a partial roll. I can still see items flying through the air, the cabin windows underwater, and Cindy, wedged in the port settee, being hit in the face with a glass jar. The jar had been ejected from its previously secure storage place and become a missile, shattering as it hit her. She was pretty stunned, and I felt I was doing a poor job of looking after the boat, let alone my new wife!

After another similar knockdown during the night, it was with some relief, early the following morning as the sky was lightening, that I re-set the tiny storm jib and got us moving again.

You can guess at how many unmeasured variables would have impacted our course and speed over that period without regular fixes: delays due to being hove to or lying ahull for several days, plus the normal influences of set and drift and leeway that we had no way of monitoring or recording, all added up to a position that could only be described as 'lost'!

At one point, when the wind and seas were down and we were enjoying a respite from the constant buffeting of heavy weather, drifting in a calm patch, Cindy was taking advantage of the easy motion and making hot chips for dinner – a rarity in the usually rocking galley – when we spotted a ship's light on the horizon. It was dusk and at first we thought we might be able to somehow get our position from them, so I altered course and even ran the little outboard in an effort to close in on their heading.

As the evening grew darker and the ship appeared to stop and we started to gain on them; after an hour or so we finally sailed up to the monster ship. We puttered alongside, immersed in the surreal glow of the high-powered deck lights. It turned out to be a fishing factory mother ship and the harsh glare of the working lights obliterated the ship's navigation lights, making it impossible to tell if they started moving again or even in which direction they might be heading.

As we irrationally sailed closer, it became obvious we were invisible to the ship – and there was no way we could communicate either, as we had no radio or ability to signal to them with lamp or flags. Turning *Deus Regit II* about, we tried to get as far away as possible, realising that this beast that we had hoped might give us some useful information could potentially run us over without even knowing we were there, let alone feeling a bump!

I was chastened and felt a bit ashamed that I had been about to give up by expecting another vessel to provide a solution to my navigation problems. My irrational approach towards the mystery ship and the stress I had been feeling was really due to a lack of confidence in my celestial navigation – a skill which I was only just getting my head around. I loved and was fascinated by the concept of making my own way across the trackless sea using the sun and moon, which can be so satisfying. But my hit-and-miss track record in the conditions we had faced had done little to give me any satisfaction. I was constantly re-reading the texts we had on board, and probably overthought the whole process. The following day Cindy spotted another smaller ship. Remembering the previous night's encounter, we gave it a wide berth.

V

Message in a Bottle

G OOD THINGS COME, as they say, to those who wait (and pray), and eventually the weather moderated, with clearing skies, as we continued edging our way east. We gradually started to turn towards a more northerly course, thankful to be moving into warmer weather, closer to the tropics. Finally we were able to get a fix by sun sights; however, the results conflicted significantly with my DR, so that I was hesitant to depend on it. I had actually been plotting at least three 'what if' scenarios based on different assumptions related to our possible course, speed, and drift, and I wasn't convinced as to the clarity of my fix, though in reality at some point you have to trust the system.

On the evening of the twenty-seventh day of the voyage, I said boldly to Cindy that by dawn we would see land – one of the Australs, a scattered group of seven islands on the southern fringe of French Polynesia. We altered course to pass within sight of a particular island which, once in view, would allow us to confirm our position. Sure enough, the following morning around dawn I was delighted to discover, exactly on schedule, an island lifting into sight over the horizon. However, its profile made it immediately apparent that it was not Ile Rurutu, which we had been expecting to see, but Ile Tubuai, which is quite different in profile and is described in the pilot book as being made up of two distinct high-peaked mountains joined by low land, appearing as two islands until you are closer. Tubuai is located 100 miles further east and a degree in latitude south of Rurutu!

This landfall – though different to what I expected – we put down to divine intervention, as the course and timing of our first sight of land was close to what I had laid off on the chart the night before – in reality it would have been easy to have missed either small island. At last we had a definite fix of our position! I was able to establish our distance off by measuring the vertical sextant angle of a known point of land (from the chart) which, combined with a compass bearing, allowed me to plot us accurately on the chart.

Later that day we sailed around the western end of Tubuai, entering the lagoon to drop the hook off a small village that was mentioned in the pilot book. The Admiralty's dry pilotage notes didn't describe the beauty. After weeks at sea the brilliant colours – varied dark and light greens of palm trees and other tropical vegetation against the turquoise waters – were invigorating. Surprisingly, a small yacht stopping off at this remote island didn't raise any interest from the locals; barely a wave was raised from some passing fishermen as they sped past in a large powered skiff. We didn't have a dinghy to get ashore, so were disappointed not to be able to meet anyone or explore the village. We spent that afternoon and evening at anchor, relaxing. We took some sights to rate my fixes in a known location, and after an easy night's sleep we sailed the next morning for Tahiti, 360 miles to our north.

Overall our small ship was doing an excellent job of looking after us. We weren't breaking any speed records, partly due to the limitations set by the self-steering method we employed. We were often forced to sail under-canvassed, but considering the fact that we had barely had to helm since leaving Australia, the balance of the boat was remarkable and speaks well of the design characteristics of the Top Hat. The class was designed in the early 1960s, for some Australian clients, by English designer John Illingworth. *Deus Regit II* was one of the fourth generation of the design, which had evolved only slightly by the time she was launched in

Dawn sighting of Tubuai – right on course, right on time, but the wrong island!

Sunset at sea, on passage to Tahiti

1986. She was built of fibreglass – some early versions were wood – and the deck and cabin profile design had been updated to appear a bit more contemporary, creating a little more internal living space. We found her to be tough and forgiving. For such a small boat she was quite dry and stable – either of which is relative, depending on the day and your perspective... but for us she was a cosy and comfortable voyaging home.

Being narrow, the Top Hat design tends to heel readily, but then the righting moment of the high-ratio lead-ballasted keel comes into play: she stiffens up and slices along nicely, making good progress for her size, with a really sweet motion – quiet and smooth, with everything working in harmony. As we sailed and got to know the boat more, we were able to maintain faster average speeds in varying conditions. In the more settled climate of the tropics, with lighter average winds and without the frequent gales, we made better time as the sheet-to-tiller steering was more often in its groove, allowing us to use maximum sail without the yawing affect and buffeting by rough seas.

We sailed this short leg to Tahiti on flat water under warm, clear skies. Navigation was easy and accurate, although the five and half days it took to cover the distance was longer than we had hoped due to unusually light trade winds.

When Tahiti was finally in sight, still over 40 miles away, Cindy wrote a note to an acquaintance – a business owner we had met in Australia before leaving – who on hearing of our wedding and upcoming voyage had requested that she send him a message in a bottle from mid-ocean as an experiment, to see where it may end up.

Cindy had been looking forward to a good moment to do this, launching an old wine bottle with a note inside. The message included a bit about ourselves and our location, that we were sailing the Australian yacht *Deus Regit II* up to Canada on our honeymoon, currently on passage between New Zealand and Tahiti. She asked the finder if they would pass the note to Don T in Newcastle, Australia, supplying the address and indicating that he would reimburse the postage to the finder. We enjoyed composing the message and thinking about where the bottle would end up, whether anyone would ever find it, and what their reaction would be.

Almost a year later, up in Canada, we were excited to hear from Don. He sent us a photocopy of a letter he had received from a young indigenous missionary student, who had found the message in the bottle washed up on the shore of the island of Epi, in Vanuatu, almost 3000 miles to the west!

Cindy launching a message in a bottle

VI

The Society Islands:
Tahiti and Moorea

R OUNDING THE WEST COAST of Tahiti, propelled by a cooperative breeze, we sailed through the reef pass and dropped anchor off Papeete town quay around midnight. We woke in the morning to find ourselves surrounded by a flotilla of pirogues (dugout canoes with outriggers) and hundreds of smiling paddlers. We had inadvertently set our anchor on the start line of the annual 74-mile marathon inter-island canoe race around Moorea. This race was part of the country's major cultural festival, celebrated on 4 July. We felt conspicuous, but no one seemed to mind as they started the race around us! (Fourteen years later, on another passage through the region, with our kids, Annie and Vance, in a much bigger boat, we arrived late at night and anchored in the same spot, coincidently on the eve of the same festival. However, with the passing of time the island had become less laid back, and we felt very unwelcome as we were publicly blasted out of the start area by race officials with huge loudspeakers. This time they had decided that we were obstructing the festivities.)

With the pirogues off and racing, the skipper of *Horizon*, an American 38-foot cutter, paddled over in his dinghy to help us reposition ourselves among the other yachts, moored only a couple of hundred metres from downtown Papeete. We set an anchor from the bow, whilst lines tied to bollards ashore held our stern towards the beach fronting the harbour shoreline.

Tahiti has always held the reputation of being an interesting and beautiful place; just the thought of it evokes images of adventure and exploration, not to mention clichéd expectations of beaches and warm tropical breezes. It was mostly true, and as this was my second passage to the magical island, I was looking forward to being able to show Cindy around Papeete.

We had been on board for 34 days, including our 22-hour stopover in Tubuai, and Cindy was excited to be in a new place and eager to get off the boat. As she changed into swimmers and was about to plunge into the water, I clumsily suggested she might want to help finish packing up the boat before we played or went ashore. In just a few words Cindy made it very clear that I needed to lighten up! It was one of the first of many lively debates we have had over the years. We are at opposite ends of the personality spectrum: I err towards the business end while she is solidly on the fun side.

During our brief time here we had work to do to prepare for the next leg of our voyage, but we also made time for fun. With the festival on all that week, the city was bustling with visitors from the outer islands. We enjoyed exploring the market, a lively hub full of traditional handcrafts and an intensely colourful array of vegetables jammed among fabrics, clothes, flowers, and less noble things like stacks of plastic buckets and brooms. The meat and seafood section provided a powerful assault on the senses. We went looking for, and rediscovered in the back streets, a fabulous patisserie that I remembered from my previous visit with George on the old *Spindrift*. French Polynesia is known as one of the most expensive countries to visit, and we felt it when stocking up for the next leg of our trip: we had only enough money to include eight oranges with our other provisions to last us about a month.

We also got to know some of the people from the eclectic mix of foreign

Deus Regit II anchored off the waterfront at Papeete

yachts that, like us, were making extended voyages – though most were heading further west in the Pacific, while our direction was north. In contrast to our recent solitude we were up late every night socialising, with invitations and visits from other yachties. The instant rapport with other cruising sailors is unique and special; a chance meeting or a shared meal can lead to a mutually enriching and encouraging encounter or be the start of a long friendship sharing experiences and ideals. You'll meet again in another port, weeks or even years later, and pick up where you left off as if no time had passed.

In the afternoon of the second day in port we received an unexpected, generous offer. Dutch-Australian Dirk Tober, the owner of *Onrust* – another boat anchored near us – had sailed single-handed in the 1950s from Europe to New Zealand, before eventually settling and raising a family in Australia and becoming a pioneer in the commercial fishing industry in the rough waters off Tasmania and Bass Strait. At the time we met him, he was part way through a circumnavigation with his wife.

Dirk had noticed Cindy and me swimming to shore, earlier in the day, with our clothes in plastic bags, and he invited us over for a coffee. Collecting us in his tender, he enquired as to where our dinghy was. After hearing the story of how it had been stolen before we left Australia, and of how we hadn't yet been able to afford to replace it, he promptly offered us a spare inflatable dinghy that had come with his boat and which, apparently, he had never had a use for. We were blown away by the offer and accepted with many thanks, only too happy to help Dirk extract the dinghy from the forward locker. It certainly made our lives simpler and drier.

Taking care of laundry on a small boat is always a challenge. One day, I was helping Cindy do our month's build-up on the beach, with an unlimited supply of fresh water from a convenient tap located at the edge of the road, immediately behind our mooring. It was typical day in paradise – warm and sunny. Cindy was working away in her bikini, while I sat on a nearby rock rinsing and wringing, when we received a visit from a local policeman. He had received complaints, and he told us that we couldn't wash our clothes there that day. It was a Sunday, and we were across the street from a large church where a traditional service was underway. Bells chimed every fifteen minutes and we could hear singing. The men wore dark formal suits and the women long white dresses and broad-brimmed hats. Meanwhile, crowds of tourists out front were taking pictures of us, hard at work!

We had thought we might attend a service, but now felt we probably wouldn't fit in with the dress code. We hadn't intended on offending anyone, so we moved further down the beach to finish our load of washing using another tap concealed by some trees. Doing laundry this way was common at the time, and the taps were provided for the boats. We certainly couldn't have afforded to pay to have our washing done. (Nowadays we would just find a laundry.)

British Columbia was still thousands of miles away, but we were determined to meet our looming deadline. We had about sixty days to sail 6000 miles. So, six days after arriving in Papeete, we cleared with customs and the port captain before sailing about fifteen miles to the island of Moorea. Here we enjoyed a quiet day and a half at anchor. We hitchhiked around the island, receiving a series of lifts from locals whose big smiles and easy laughter made us feel welcome, even though we couldn't speak much French or Tahitian. Cook's Bay, named for its association with the famed navigator who first visited in 1769 and also known as Pao-Pao Bay, is one of the South Pacific's quintessential anchorages – a visual feast, complete with jagged mountain peaks and a deep, sheltered lagoon, with palm trees and foliage extending down to the water. Even though there are villages and houses ashore, it feels like you are in a protected amphitheatre of peace and quiet.

Cindy in Cook's Bay – Moorea quickly became a favourite destination

VII

Across the Equator
to Hawaii

W E SAILED NORTH FROM MOOREA on the tail end of a rare southerly gale, taking advantage of these fresh breezes to shoot further into the tropics. For three days we averaged 120 miles a day – great progress and an encouraging start – before the wind eased and our 24-hour runs dropped off.

Once clear of some atolls near our track, we headed north-east almost as far as the Marquesas before turning directly north. Our aim was to make as much easting as possible before crossing the equator, then continue due north for another 600 miles so that we could catch the trade winds to Hilo, on the Big Island of Hawaii. This plan worked to a T and we made good time, covering just shy of 3000 miles in 30 days – a much better average than we experienced during the southern passage from New Zealand to Tahiti.

Just before leaving Papeete we had heard of the schooner *Sea Swan*, sailed by an old friend, Miles Courtner. Miles was an acclaimed artist and had been sailing the world since he'd built the boat in the late 1960s. I had first met him on a previous trip to New Zealand and Tahiti, in 1981. We had just missed seeing *Sea Swan* in Moorea, Miles having left a day or so before we arrived, bound, like us, for Hawaii.

Miles was a ham radio enthusiast – as so many cruisers are – and he logged in each day to one of the Pacific maritime mobile radio nets. Aboard *Deus Regit* we didn't have a transmitter, but we could tune in to the ham radio frequency on our short-wave receiver to listen to other yachts which were traversing different areas of the Pacific. It provided a sense of community, knowing we weren't the only ones out there, and it helped us get a perspective on weather patterns.

We had enjoyed dialling in and listening most evenings on the leg to Tahiti, but on this passage it felt more personal, knowing that Miles was sailing ahead of us on *Sea Swan*, following basically the same route. It became a fun daily event to record and plot *Sea Swan*'s progress relative to ours. While we couldn't expect to keep up with the much larger 53-foot yacht, it was helpful having a benchmark and hearing about the weather conditions they encountered crossing the equator and the doldrums as they headed into the Northern Hemisphere. Miles had no idea we were in the area, nipping at his heels.

We sailed for 13 days to reach the equator – and crossing it was another first for both of us, and a cause for celebration. The traditional equatorial rite of passage in the days of commercial sailing called for novice crew to be smeared with a ghastly concoction of grease and food scraps and dunked in the sea – probably on a bosun's chair, or at the end of a length of rope – or some other form of humiliation inflicted by the veteran crew. We were fortunate in being equal first timers so there was no one qualified to mete out such a punishment. Our festivities took on a more civilised tone.

Cindy prepared a feast fit for the occasion – an Asian dish with rice – followed by the crowd-pleaser of canned Christmas pudding supplied by her grandmother and saved for the event. We devoured it topped with hot, freshly made custard, restraining ourselves just enough to have leftovers for the next day. It might sound like a rather simple meal, but compared to our usual fare, and combined with the pleasure of anticipation, it amplified the satisfaction we enjoyed in marking the milestone. In the right place, at the right time, with the best company!

Another beautiful sunrise at sea. One of the reasons we go!

I really enjoyed this leg: we made steady progress and the weather was consistently light to moderate. Even crossing the doldrums in near calm conditions, we trickled along with relatively healthy daily runs of 40, 60, and 80 miles. Once into the north-east trades we made much better time, in fresher reaching winds, with *Deus Regit II*, unfettered, averaging 110–130 miles per day.

Cindy, on the other hand, found the hot tropical days repetitive and boring. The sun and heat on deck were merciless; the small cabin was stuffy, hot, and humid. To create some shade and make conditions more tolerable on deck during the day, we rigged a poly tarp over the cockpit and dodger, tied down to the lifelines.

Cindy started to think that the previous leg hadn't been so bad – at least there was more activity! Down south we had a significant weather change every 12 hours, or so it seemed. We were constantly trimming and fiddling with the sail–helm equilibrium, with each variation of pressure, sail combination, or pounding from the restless seas. In the heat, I think we both forgot how cold and rough it had been just a few weeks before. I was rattled when Cindy actually voiced the idea of opting out of the last leg and flying to Canada to wait for me to join her!

This dissatisfaction on Cindy's part may have been due to fatigue. We had met, married, and left Australia within a period of 10 weeks, and our pace across the Pacific so far, while not fast in terms of pure boat speed, had been hectic. Relentless concentration was required to remain focused on the job at hand and looming seasonal and other deadlines. The accumulated stress of dealing with the vagaries of the weather, combined with the physical effort of being on a small boat for an extended period of time, with only snatches of broken sleep, and with a poor diet all took their toll on her.

Even while sleeping, on a boat your body is tense and your muscles are working, holding you in the bunk. When you are awake, the continual motion conspires to wear you down. It was easier for me, as I had been doing it for longer: it was my drive and interest that had set the pace, whereas Cindy had been making adjustments from day one – learning a new sailing language, dealing with an unfamiliar and often harsh environment, and not least living with this bloke she had known for only a short while and had no possibility of avoiding!

An extract from her journal at the time speaks of her frustration, and is a far cry from her usual positive self. It picks up when we had been at sea for about three weeks. Usually, Cindy made comprehensive notes of what happened each day, until these brief entries:

2 August, Sunday: Same as yesterday. Getting very bored. Still sailing well though?

3 August, Monday: Still sailing well, still bored ...

7 August, Friday: Running out of things to eat now ... have basic meals organised till Monday ... I am tired of reading, listening to the radio, and watching the clock. My bottom is numb from sitting. The time goes very slow ... All I can do is wait and wait and wait. We were going to get in on Monday, but as usual it now looks like Tuesday or Wednesday. It seems that when you get to the end of the rope you find it is only longer. I am writing this down so I can look back and thank God for what I learnt – even if I can't see it at the moment. I can't cook anything from the recipe books as you need to bake it or cool it, and we have no oven and no fridge. NO washing machine, no shower, no comfortable seat ... There is a nice view. The moon is bright and we see lots of stars most of the time. There is NO bath to soak your feet in. NO water to wash with. I couldn't care less ... I look terrible; I can't wash my hair properly ...

Later we learnt that Cindy's health had suffered during this time: she had become malnourished and anaemic – early signs of scurvy. We had little money, and in our inexperience we probably hadn't managed the balance between economy and nutrition very well. The short stopovers and minimal time for recovery had had a damaging effect on Cindy's physical well-being.

Saying that, it wasn't all doom and gloom. We both loved the late afternoons and evenings when the sun's intensity had eased. Rolling back the tacky plastic temporary awning to enjoy the view, we would eat in the cockpit and spend hours talking and gazing at the night sky, feeling blessed to be there, and realising what an extraordinary experience we were sharing.

My navigation was falling into place each day, with a nice string of consecutive noon fixes, the accuracy of which I attributed to the milder conditions. It was pleasant, and knowing where we were certainly reduced the pressure on us, however I still had an interesting challenge in this regard.

As we progressed north, the sun's declination was moving south towards us with the change of season, until for a few days we were at a point passing directly underneath it. This meant that the sights I was taking in the morning were on the same (east) or reciprocal (west) azimuth as my noon sights and afternoon sights, making it impossible for the position lines to cross for a fix. This phenomenon is something you have to deal with occasionally, but it was the first time I had experienced it. I was scratching my head as to how to get an accurate fix.

My research drew me to a comment in a book by Eric Hiscock, in which he mentioned the same thing occurring on a passage for him and Susan. He described a method of obtaining 'very high altitude sights'. I persisted in following his instructions, in an effort to get a fix, but it was complicated and I didn't feel confident in the outcome. However, later we were able to use the moon to get sights that agreed with our reckoning. It was an interesting exercise, but I was happy to see the sun finally pass south of us and become a useful nav aid once again.

By the time we were due to make landfall, we were eager to arrive and have a break. I worked on an ETA of 4:00 p.m., but as we approached the coast of the Big Island of Hawaii we sailed into low, dense, tropical cloud and heavy rain. Visibility was obscured to the point that we were unable to locate any definitive landmarks to pinpoint our position, so we stopped the boat and hove to for the night. Some vague shore lights became visible later in the night, and before dawn the low cloud started to lift. We sighted a navigation mark that allowed us to establish our course and distance left to run. With renewed excitement at another successful landfall, we made sail and arrived mid-morning into Radio Bay, the breakwater harbour for Hilo.

VIII

Hawaii

ENTERING RADIO BAY, the port captain met us in a launch and directed us to anchor with stern lines ashore along the inner sea wall. US customs authorities were a bit rattled that we had arrived without visas. We didn't need them for New Zealand or Tahiti, and with our recent pace of life we hadn't given it much thought. But somehow they tolerated our lack of planning and checked us in without too much fuss, after which we collected a big pile of mail from the port captain's office.

It was about 5 kilometres to the city business area and, keen to catch the banks, I hitched a ride to town to change some money I'd received in the mail. Going into a store to buy a can of soda, I was surprised when the guy who had given me a ride sidled up beside me and silently placed a carton of beer on the counter; it was clear he expected me to pay for it. Not really having any choice, I did. It turned out to be pretty good value, as later in the day he offered to take us back to collect some groceries, and this time only demanded a bag of peanuts!

Another time, Cindy and I accepted a lift in a car occupied by a few wild-looking people. We were more than a little intimidated when they demanded money at the end of the ride or they wouldn't let us out of the car. It felt a bit like the Wild West; taxis were starting to look like a better option!

In Hilo we again lined up for another round of hectic socialising, including with Miles on *Sea Swan*. He was berthed near us and we connected easily with the other cruising sailors; we were familiar with some of the yacht names, having heard them check in on the ham radio networks. Miles remembered me and was very welcoming, and delighted to meet Cindy. We shared some meals and even a movie night on board *Sea Swan* – a rare thing to be able to do back then.

Don and Debbie, a local couple we met through a mutual contact in Papeete, were incredibly kind and helpful. We phoned to introduce ourselves and made arrangements for them to call by the following morning. They arrived bearing flowers and a tray of freshly baked brownies, and were accompanied by another couple visiting from California. They took time out to show us around the island, and drove us to their beautiful home up in the hills overlooking the city, leaving us free reign to relax and luxuriate in hot showers and the great view for a few hours while they went to take care of some work. We felt undeservedly spoilt.

Don took it upon himself to check in on us most days. He would swing by the boat after enjoying his early morning surf at a nearby break, to ask if we needed a lift or if there was anything he could help with.

Towards the end of our stay, Don and Debbie kindly drove us to the markets so we could restock for the next leg. We had arrived in Hilo with our supplies reduced to a few cans of kidney beans and a handful or two of rice. We'd also spent all our money in Tahiti, leaving with only a few Pacific Franc coins, equal to a few Australian cents. (We still have those coins on a shelf in our library!) Luckily, in Hilo we both received money from our annual tax rebates, so at that moment we were probably the richest we had been since knowing each other. We took advantage of the situation while in the land of milk and honey to stock up on a great quantity and variety of healthy ingredients for the next leg. Fortunately, money went much further in the US than in expensive Tahiti, where the selection of food products had also been limited.

We enjoyed generous hopsitality as we were shown the Big Island Hawaii

A significant advantage of cruising in the Top Hat was that it was quite low maintenance. We never arrived in port with a huge job list of things to do or fix. We were enjoying a pretty reliable, cost-effective little ship. However, I did make one important discovery during a routine inspection of the rig a few days before we were set to leave Hilo: a few wire strands in the stainless steel forestay had cracked. Fortunately this was visible at the lower end of the headsail-furling unit. To discover this damage to such an important piece of rigging a week or two into the trip would have been a nuisance, if not a disaster, with the real possibility of a dismasting. However, after a few hours' effort using some borrowed tools, the next day the repaired wire was back in place and safe for departure.

In view of the difficulties I'd had navigating, we decided it was time to invest in some better nav equipment. I purchased a new sextant from West Marine in California, to be delivered the day before departure. My old sextant was an Ebbco plastic model designed as a backup device to be carried in ships' lifeboats; it wasn't really intended for everyday use. I had bought the instrument by mail order when I was a kid, with the intention of practising and learning the principles of celestial navigation, and it was well past its use-by date. The small, poor-quality mirrors were badly corroded by salt and spray, affecting its accuracy. It was partly responsible for my lack of precision on the rougher southern legs.

Navigation was going to need to be spot on for this leg into the North Pacific. All reports indicated we could expect a high frequency of heavy fog, especially towards the end of the passage as we closed with the coast.

Leaving Hilo after a refreshing 12 days, we looked forward to the final portion north to British Columbia. (Yes, Cindy forgot about her earlier desire to sit out this leg of the voyage.) It wasn't that we were eager for our voyage to end, but we were keen to embark on the next stage of the journey – the reason for our imminent deadline.

The year before, I had booked to attend a Bible College located on Thetis Island – one of the Gulf Islands grouped between the mainland city of Vancouver and Vancouver Island. The plan to attend the college gave additional focus and purpose to the task of fitting out *Deus Regit II* for the voyage. The start date for the course was only three weeks away, and although we had no hope of making that date, we wanted to arrive as close as possible in order to keep up with the classes over the coming winter. I didn't see our late arrival as a negative, considering we had started the voyage 12 weeks later than I had originally planned – the fact that I was now arriving with Cindy more than made up for the delay.

IX

North Pacific Ocean to Canada

T HE TRADITIONAL ROUTE from Hawaii to Canada or the West Coast of the USA was to sail due north, around the back of the clockwise-rotating North Pacific High, avoiding the area of calms and light winds in the centre of that vast area of dynamic high pressure. Once on top of this system, westerly winds in the higher latitudes would helpfully push us towards our destination. We weren't reinventing the wheel – many ships and yachts had sailed this route before – but I wasn't aware of many 25-footers making the passage. The voyage would take us up to 48 degrees north latitude, with at least another month at sea before making landfall.

It was hard to leave the good weather of the tropics, especially as we would be heading towards winter. Friends suggested we find an alternative Bible school in the islands and spend the winter in Hawaii. This was not such a bad idea, and there was one on the island – but it was not part of our plan, so we cast off, with our long-held goal of a successful Pacific crossing intact, sailing from Radio Bay on 24 August 1987.

The first day out was fantastic sailing. North-east trade winds tending more east than north enabled us to make great time, on course, only heeling slightly in flat seas as the miles ticked effortlessly by. By noon the next day we had made good 112 miles in less than 24 hours. We followed this good progress with two more consecutive days' runs of just over 125 miles each, and it felt like *Deus Regit II*, with a bone in her teeth, was intent on getting us up to Canada on time for the study year to begin. However, it's never healthy to start thinking about ETAs too early in a voyage.

Not long into this leg, we began to notice lots of flotsam in the ocean. It seemed that whenever we looked about we would spot objects in the water, and each day we would see something different, from a plastic bucket that once held bulk peanut butter (labelled, and with apparent remnants inside) to long lengths of heavy synthetic line, which may have had their origins in the fishing industry. One afternoon we spotted the reflection from a rare 30-centimetre-diameter Japanese glass fishing float and, altering course, we sailed over and retrieved it. (This area has since become known as the North Pacific Gyre or Garbage Patch. It is the area where the currents converge and marine debris accumulate in the area, creating a huge collection of flotsam and rubbish that increases with each year as rubbish is washed out to sea from Japan, Asia, and North America.)

Later we found a smaller 100-millimetre-diameter float. I had never seen one this size before. It was odd to come across these seemingly fragile glass spheres, made of rough blown glass. There was no way of knowing how long they had been adrift, but it was good to know that modest size and watertightness can be a safe combination – something we relied on, living aboard our small yacht!

All too soon the wind dropped off, becoming light and blowing from astern. Running with our usual downwind setup – the mainsail braced out one side, and, opposite it, the genoa extending on an aluminium pole like a wing to catch the fickle breeze – we ambled through a slow 80 miles, then a dismal 47-mile run before the wind swung through 180 degrees to come from ahead.

I was not expecting, nor happy about, the headwinds. We were forced to beat to windward for the first time in over 7000 miles! It was a moderate breeze – less than 20 knots – but the seas became lumpy, unsettling our unfamiliar tummies. The situation was not too dire, as the chop was only small. We knew conditions would change in our favour at some point, and so we plugged away for about 72 hours, heeled well over, making the best course and speed that we could.

One afternoon we sighted a large ship and enjoyed watching for some time as it altered course to check us out, steaming up beside us. We could not communicate with the tanker *Arco Texas*, but it felt good to see another vessel. Somehow, knowing that they had seen us gave us a connection to the rest of the planet; it was a companionable and kind gesture that they had deliberately merged with our course, though leaving plenty of room. It would have been nice to speak with the watch on board, but with no VHF radio that was impossible. We were sure of our position so there was no urgency; we waved them on and returned to our isolation as they brought the ship back up to speed and resumed course, we guessed for Alaska.

Each day our sightings of flotsam continued with amazing consistency. One morning I noticed a rusty industrial gas or oxygen bottle floating nearby. It resembled a sawn-off torpedo covered with gooseneck barnacles, and I was glad we didn't bump into it during the night! The following day, Cindy spotted what appeared to be a large timber hatch-cover with a big brown bird perched on it like a sentinel drifting on the calm sea.

On day ten the wind freed again, letting us ease the sheets slightly and sail a more direct course to the north. Arriving at the targeted latitude of 40 degrees north on day sixteen, the breeze switched, almost like clockwork, coming out of the west right on schedule. This new wind signalled that we had successfully circumvented the area of light winds in the high-pressure zone. We altered course to a more north-easterly direction, putting us on the home straight and on the lay line for Cape Flattery, 1500 miles distant. This was certainly a high point. At last we were heading towards the mark we had been thinking about for so long.

The 40 degrees north point also marked half way for the passage. We celebrated this key milestone with a special evening meal created by Cindy from our meagre stores. We had chicken with roast potatoes, followed by strawberries and canned cream. Cindy had the knack of making simple dishes taste out of this world, and we often enjoyed fresh bread baked in a pressure cooker on the alcohol stove, or even cakes, baked in the pan or pressure cooker with amazing success. I was always impressed.

Overall, this leg was progressing well. Our tactic of finding favourable westerlies had paid off, and we were making good time. By now we had been at sea for more than twenty days and were well into the higher latitudes near 45° N. The swell and westerly winds had increased significantly, and it was a great deal colder than only a few days earlier, when we were still under the influence of the North Pacific High. We were starting to rug up and to make use of our small heater, purchased in Hilo. This consisted of a simple metal bucket with wadding in it, into which you poured alcohol and lit it. Fire in a bucket – I can't imagine anyone doing that these days!

Gradually the winds built to gale force, and we maintained our habit of monitoring weather daily by tuning in to radio station WWVH. Broadcasting from Hawaii, WWVH transmits on the 5, 10, and 15 MHz frequencies on the short-wave band, sending out the constant beep-beep-beeeep of time signals 24 hours a day. This allowed us to synchronise our watches to Coordinated Universal Time (UTC or GMT), which we needed for accurate celestial navigation. Another important, though perhaps meagre, thing we relied on from WWVH was weather informa-tion. At the 48–51-minute period after the hour, the high seas forecast of weather warnings was announced for the entire North Pacific. It was a dense amount of information, and we had to listen carefully to glean the details related to our spe-cific ocean region, plotting the fronts and low-pressure systems as they tracked towards us.

Listening quietly to the short-wave radio one morning after a rough night at sea, I heard the disconnected, electronic voice of the broadcaster confirming that the gale was intensifying. We could expect winds of 50 knots or more – and big seas! I was hesitant to relay this to Cindy, curled up on the end of the settee with her legs folded under her. But seeing the tension in my face as I broke the news of the probable storm-force winds and 25-foot seas, she remained stoic. "Only 50 knots," she said, sounding almost relieved, "that's not so bad... and there's noth-ing we can do about that." She was right of course.

This first really big blow came from the west and north-west, so we were able to hold our course, though progress was reduced in the rougher conditions. We sailed through the night with just the staysail set. In the morning it was blowing well over 40 knots as I tied a reef into that small sail for the first time. For two days we sailed with only a tiny scrap of canvas. Again and again we were knocked down, several times by breaking seas, before the wind eased, leaving us rolling in a big swell.

We enjoyed a respite of little more than a day of lighter wind before another gale kicked in, this time from the south. We sailed fast for a while, broad-reaching in winds well over 35 knots with heavily reefed main and jib, until the new sea state became unruly. Progressively reducing sail area, we slogged on like this from 15 to 17 September, until we were riding it out under bare poles for several hours in the night. By morning we were relieved to welcome a soft west-north-westerly breeze.

Soon under full sail again, in the lighter conditions we aired the cabin, and were able to partially dry out our water-soaked bunk cushions. (We had developed a small leak from the anchor locker drain – not dangerous but certainly annoying, as it soaked our forward bunk mattress.) During the day, the breeze shifted to come more from the south, increasing, and continued to back to the south-east and resume blowing at full gale force.

You would think that storms at sea would be fully locked down under heavy black clouds – and that is often the case. But the following morning, as I worked on deck to put the reef in the staysail, the wind was tearing the tops off the huge waves and *Deus Regit II* was getting pummelled like never before, yet we had a sparkling bright blue sky and sea. The contrast between the wind-driven spray and white foaming crests against the deep, dark blue of the ocean was beautiful, though ominous.

We plodded along at a couple of knots on our east-north-easterly heading, with the winds mostly from the south-east to south-west – indicating that the storm system was moving to the north and west of us. With the main down and lashed firmly to the boom, we had set only the tiny staysail – under which the boat was surprisingly still able to self-steer, with the helm lashed loosely and the tiller free to move about a bit, finding its own groove. Later, as the wind eased – though still above gale force – we unrolled part of the clew of the furled genoa. This small increase of sail area made a dramatic difference to our speed and, defying logic, it seemed to balance with the staysail to keep the boat moving close to the proper course without our help.

We were still able to get sun sights and work up a noon position on all but one day during this passage; so the new sextant had been worth its weight in gold, with its larger mirrors and the silver intact! Even though this new sextant was also plastic, it was a more stable instrument made by Davis and it better tolerated the changes in temperature which had often noticeably influenced the Ebbco model we had previously been depending on.

This major weather system, which had started influencing us 200 miles ahead of the front, grew to cover an expanse more than 1000 miles wide, with 40–50-knot winds and 25-foot-plus seas, before starting to diminish about three days later.

As the storm began to ease we tentatively raised more sail, shaking out one reef at a time. After several days at the mercy of the rough conditions it felt liberating to finally be able to take a more active stance in making our way towards our landfall on Cape Flattery. At this point we had just over 300 miles to go. Overhead we spotted an aircraft, given away by its gleaming contrail and appearing to be, like us, on track for British Columbia.

Nearing the coast with a waning breeze, we finally ran into the dreaded fog we had heard so much about. Now we drifted gently on a slate-grey sea, under a similarly coloured sky – such muted colours compared to the recent storm's brilliant cobalt blue. Navigation was getting serious, and we would soon see how accurate we had been with our sights. As they say, "Your last fix is the one that matters!"

Sailing in fog is quite surreal. In light airs there is no real reference point:

you're gliding in an ill-defined sphere of grey, seemingly suspended in a merged sea and sky with limited sensory input. Yet in this silent beauty, you're on high alert, aware of the dangerous risk of collision.

Snatching glimpses of the veiled sun through the misty canopy, we managed to maintain our daily noon plots. About 80 miles from the coast, we used a radio direction-finding (RDF) device to help determine our position. Craig and Marsha, cruisers on *Gaia* whom we had met in Hawaii, had insisted that we should take their device to have on hand for the tricky landfall, and then mail it back to them from Canada. Radio beacon signals from Tofino and another station on Vancouver Island, crossed with an earlier sun line, confirmed our position, enabling us to confidently make our approach to Cape Flattery.

RDFs have been around since before World War II, but the device felt sophisticated and high tech compared to our simple manual navigation methods. The RDF enabled us, when in range of the beacons, to monitor our position regardless of visibility and time of day. This was fortunate and much appreciated, as we had been forced south by coastal currents; with the RDF we could check our position regularly and compensate accordingly to make a near-perfect landfall.

We soon began to see signs that we were nearing land. Large amounts of kelp floated by, and we dodged a huge log that must have been discharged from a coastal waterway. Shipping traffic also increased, and we started to see large, heavily laden

Cindy using the Radio Direction Finder to pinpoint our position as we make landfall at Cape Flattery

container ships heading out on random paths to destinations unknown. So far on this leg from Hawaii there had been little animal life, but now we had a surprising visit from a March fly and, to our awe and delight, a killer whale (orca) cruised around the boat. Later some Dall's porpoises gambolled around us, initially with dramatic effect as their colouring is similar to the orca; but ultimately a welcome, friendly escort.

Our arrival was a significant achievement: we had been married for only five months, and in that time had navigated the vast width of the world's largest ocean, facing numerous challenges along the way. Cindy and I were getting to know each other well, and we had learnt many lessons together. *Deus Regit II* had been in the water less than 10 months and had looked after us, never letting us down in a real mixed bag of conditions during 115 days at sea and almost 10,000 miles. Keeping up this relentless schedule was testimony to her reliability and solid sea-keeping qualities.

After clearing Cape Flattery we had less than 100 miles to sail through the Strait of Juan de Fuca to Victoria, British Columbia, where we could officially enter Canada. It was taxing to be suddenly sailing within the narrow constraints of the strait, with busy lines of shipping entering and leaving at speed. Strong winds funnelling into the strait, combined with the vagaries of heavy tidal streams and currents, made this one of the most challenging parts of the voyage. We had spent the afternoon tied up in Neah Bay, a few miles inside the entrance on the American side, to wait for a suitable tide to help us on the final overnight leg to Victoria.

I was kept on my toes navigating, ship spotting and, as the capricious wind was gusting near gale force from astern, hand steering. At one point during the night, we had to cross the 12-mile-wide strait to the Canadian side to reach more favourable currents. I aimed to cross astern of the lights of one large vessel, thinking we would have plenty of room ahead of the next ship in line. But with my hands full, we ended up in front of the next freighter barrelling towards us. We were crossing the strait and traffic flow at a 90-degree angle, as required – but the incoming tidal stream was pushing us sideways and, combined with the ship's advancing speed, the gap between us was closing uncomfortably fast. With the wind now on the beam, we were also heeled over sharply in the uncomfortable choppy waters, with leeway also cutting into our safety margin. In the pitch-black night I feared they would not see us, despite our radar reflector aloft in the rigging.

It quickly became apparent that I had cut it too fine, and I was doing everything I could to speed up. I felt that *Deus Regit II* was digging deep also, to help out. It was close, but we were going to be okay. The approaching ship's red and green running lights were in agreement with her mast lights, confirming that we had passed from one side to the other, though still too close. Even so, I was glad Cindy was asleep below – or at least, so I thought!

Unbeknown to me, Cindy had woken as I altered course and the boat's motion changed in the slop. For some time she had been perched on the edge of the dinette settee below, tension building as she watched the dark bow of the massive ship looming over us through the cabin window. Convinced that we were about to be run down, she surprised me by rushing up from below screaming that she "hadn't sailed all the way across the Pacific only for you to kill us both at the end of it!" I tried to calm her by saying we were okay and clear, but she had had such a fright that it took her a while to settle down. She was pretty upset with me.

Once on the other side and back on course, with the wind firmly behind us, we scooted off up the strait, hugging the Canadian shoreline well out of range of any other monster ships. But Cindy decided she'd had enough and left me to it. I didn't see her for the rest of the night.

Later, as daylight was breaking and we were nearing the turn at Race Rocks for the last 10 miles into port, she came up on deck feeling more sociable, having recovered from her fright. We sailed the last part together, enjoying the morning and the view in company. Vancouver Island was close on our port side and, further away on the mainland, distant snowy mountain peaks were framed against a brilliant blue autumn sky.

No other boats were on the water except for what looked like an old brigantine. We later came to know her as the recently launched *Spirit of Chemainus*, a sail training vessel for the SALTS organisation set up to teach young people sailing and life skills.

Docking in front of the famous Edwardian-era Empress Hotel, in this peaceful, sheltered harbour, seemed to bookend the trip nicely. We were elated to be there and to have successfully completed the voyage. It was a small achievement on a world scale, but the sense of accomplishment was deeply satisfying for us, having been focused for so long on reaching Canada. We enjoyed that great feeling that comes when you complete a passage of any length; but this was a little more significant, as we had traversed the full width of the Pacific Ocean. Of course we were aware that we were 15 days late to start our studies, but we reckoned we had earned a weekend off.

Catching our breath for a few days in Victoria, we cleared customs and sorted the paperwork for the boat and our study visas. Our red Australian ensign flying off the backstay attracted attention from other yachties. As the city marina was open to the public, we even had to field questions from passers-by who, walking the docks admiring the boats, had noticed that *Deus Regit II* was registered in Australia. One character even asked if we had flown the boat over or sent it on a ship!

The next morning about dawn, my sleep was interrupted as I felt the boat moving silently through the water. Ducking out into the cockpit, I was astonished to see that two crew from a newly arrived large yacht had untied our dock lines and shoved us from our berth – and no one said a word! *Deus Regit II* drifted the short distance across the u-shaped marina pen to settle gently on a shorter section of dock. The bigger vessel immediately commandeered our original, more convenient berth alongside the pontoon. I jumped to the dock, cleated off our lines and slid back into bed. I guess the other crew would have retied our lines if I hadn't surfaced from below...?

The comfortable marina offered a relaxed life and social scene and we enjoyed meeting locals and other sailors, many over from the nearby US San Juan Islands and from other places in BC. However, we knew we would have to tear ourselves away for the final leg of the trip, and we began our preparations.

We only had about 40 miles to go to reach Thetis Island, where the Bible College was located. We split the trip over two days and enjoyed the novelty of day sailing, piloting through passes and narrows among the Gulf Islands. With no wind, and being so far from the ocean, we motored in absolutely flat water, sheltered all around by pine-forested islands. Navigation was relaxed, with plenty of landmarks in sight.

As we drifted into the small bay on Thetis Island, we felt a sense of completion, together with anticipation – a new chapter in our lives was about to begin! Moored alongside the solitary floating dock off the front lawn of the Capernwray Harbour Bible College, our destination for that season, we felt a little conspicuous tidying up on deck. A small group of people wandered down the lawns towards us to see if we were, in fact, the long-awaited Aussie sailors they had been hearing about.

X

Life in Canada – and the Unexpected Happens!

WE LOVED LIVING IN BRITISH COLUMBIA. It had a clean, unspoilt environment and beautiful, sheltered waterways with easily accessible gunkholes. Because we had stopped moving, it became a home base that we shared and developed together. We made some enduring friendships as a couple; before leaving Australia each of us had had our own friends, with few mutual friends, and although we made good connections with people at sea, they were understandably transitory.

Our college experience was rewarding and two years passed quickly. But it was certainly a big change for us, after the solitude of sailing, to be suddenly living with more than eighty other students and having to fit into a rigid schedule of classes, study, and community life.

For eight months we lived ashore, leaving *Deus Regit II* moored about 200 metres away at a small marina in the perfectly sheltered Telegraph Harbour. It was freezing cold for our unacclimatised Aussie bodies, fresh from the tropics, and with the busy college timetable it was more convenient (and warmer!) to live on campus.

While there, I had access to the school's cabinet-makers' workshop and tools, so was able to do some refitting in the interior of the boat which later improved life and order for us. I built some useful cupboards and alcove-style book shelves in the main cabin in place of what had previously been a long, open-top shelf. This made down below feel cosier, and the improved storage system was also safer – objects were less likely to be hurled about the cabin during the rough spells we occasionally experienced at sea.

The following May, after completing the study program, we exchanged our student visas for work permits and moved back on board. *Deus Regit II* was due for her first

The cabin where we lived at Capernwray Harbour Bible College

haul-out and fresh bottom paint, so we sailed to another small harbour, in Maple Bay on Vancouver Island, where there were marine and boat-building facilities.

When we arrived at Maple Bay we didn't have a firm plan beyond slipping the boat, but it proved to be a fantastic base and was to become our home for the rest of our time in Canada. It was convenient, finding work was easy and, as well as gaining experience boat building, I could work on our boat using the available tools, skills, and supplies. It was still in the area of Thetis Island and the friends we had made there, and we met many other interesting people.

We also got to know the region better. We bought an old Toyota for $300, to get about in and explore further afield on land. When time permitted we sailed as far south as Seattle, at the head of Puget Sound, and, closer to home, we explored the other nearby Gulf Islands and the US San Juan Islands. Cruising a little further 'up island', as it was called, we day-hopped north along Vancouver Island's forested and ruggedly beautiful coastline, with its rich marine and bird life. The sea eagles especially were always fascinating.

In our part of Australia we mostly enjoy fairly benign tidal conditions. British Columbia, like many areas of the world, experiences tidal extremes and associated big currents churn through the myriad narrow channels and cuts between islands. With only an outboard for auxiliary power, we had to plan ahead to use these strong movements of water; the alternative was to slug it out, going nowhere or even backwards, as happened to us once when entering Porlier Pass between Galliano and Valdez Islands.

We had aimed for slack water, but arrived about fifteen minutes late. We knew there was only a small window of slack but, expecting it to still be okay, we charged in, motoring flat out at 6 knots. About a third of the way through the gap between the two islands our bow poked into a slight swirl of water mid-channel – and our whole world changed as we were forcefully ejected in reverse from the pass, travelling at about 4 knots over the ground, although our engine was still powering fast forward!

This experience taught us that planning was key and that it was often more expedient to anchor behind a headland, or tuck into a small cove, to wait for the change in tidal direction. We could gain back the time with a free lift from a favourable tide a bit later in the day. After a while we got used to playing the tides to advantage, and we enjoyed this challenging aspect of navigation and the satisfaction of getting it right.

We had arrived in Maple Bay with very little money. I introduced myself to Phil Pidcock, the owner of the boatyard, Cove Yachts, and told him what we had been up to, and that we were in need of a haul out and some general maintenance. I boldly asked if he would consider letting us work on his hard standing for a few days, to take care of our list of jobs, and also allow me a few weeks to pay our yard bill, once I had found a job.

Smiling and tilting his head back, Phil nodded a thoughtful yes, kindly agreeing to extend us some credit. We slipped the boat there, repainted the antifouling, and took care of some wear and tear that needed attention after more than 10,000 miles and a year and a half in the water. *Deus Regit II* seemed relieved and looked better for some love.

After we had been in the yard a few days, Phil ambled over one morning and stood quietly beside me. Never one to be called a chatterbox, he mumbled into his beard, "You can work here if you want." So that was that; I had a job and we had a great location to live and work. I guess it also guaranteed that Phil and Sandra, his wife, would get the yard bill paid! We had a one-year visa and wanted to save as much as we could before heading south to the USA, where we would be unable to get work visas.

Cove Yachts was rife with know-how. Phil had been trained as a shipwright at the famous Hilliard Boatbuilders in southern England, and there were five other guys working in the yard, most of whom were experienced offshore sailors. Winston was a local legend who had already circumnavigated with his family. Shortly after we were there, he skippered the first Canadian private expedition yacht to traverse the Northwest Passage. Thom Reidl, a Canadian who had become a shipwright in New Zealand after a successful career as a commercial photographer, brought an artisan's flair to boat-building. He inspired me with his commitment to detail and his enthusiasm. Thom and his wife Kath became close friends; they had sailed to BC from New Zealand aboard their self-built yacht *Katie II* the season after we arrived, and were living aboard nearby.

The yard was a compact but busy place, and took on a variety of jobs on all manner of craft – from big, tough local fishing boats to modern yachts. We even undertook some interesting wooden sailboat restoration projects. The 100-ton slipway could handle boats to about 90 feet in length, and a gantry crane was used to lift smaller vessels onto the concrete hard-standing area, where we lifted *Deus Regit II*.

Cindy and I enjoyed life at Cove Marina. We were docked part way down the left side of the long central pier with a variety of yachts on fingers either side. I could get to work in about 30 seconds, which suited me as I didn't have to rise too early, and the showers and washing machine on site made it convenient. Though there were no shops close by, everything we needed was a 15-minute drive away in Duncan, the large town that served the region. Cindy soon found jobs with a local yacht charter company and the post office in Duncan. We integrated, feeling like locals.

I took the opportunity to make some more modifications to the boat; Cindy was keen to have an oven, something which until that point hadn't crossed my mind. We purchased a used one that had started life on the solid teak 50-foot *Chevalier*, built in Hong Kong and originally sailed from the UK to BC via the Panama Canal. Clifford, the octogenarian owner, maintained the boat with clear-coat varnished topsides and was tearing into it with the energy of a much younger man, re-caulking deck seams and doing his own refit, including an upgrade to his galley.

We took a grinder to our small galley, chopping out most of the original fibreglass module, creating space for the gimballed propane stove and oven. It was a major modification to our galley, where the old two-burner alcohol stove had been accessed by reaching behind the moulded fibreglass sink to a space crammed under the side deck. Besides the new cooker, we extended the counter top, repositioning and replacing the white fibreglass sink with a sparkling stainless steel one. It made a big difference to the overall look and provided more practical working space.

Now we had plenty of work area, with extra counter tops, a nice easy-to-clean stainless steel sink, a gas oven, and a stove, with new lockers behind. Overall it was a civilised set-up for such a small yacht, efficiently using the space. Overhead, we fitted an opening hatch that provided ventilation and light for the galley.

It seems every waterway in the world is home to an eclectic mix of characters living on boats. Cove Marina was no exception, and we enjoyed getting to know the interesting 'liveaboards' on the dock near us. Our nearest neighbours were a couple, Duck and Gaye, long-term liveaboards on a 32-foot Westsail double-ender. He was a retired pathologist and an avid gun collector, with a preference for wearing camouflage fatigues – surely a conspiracy theorist! Duck kept to himself, barely speaking with anyone – though, typically, Cindy eventually won him over. Being a cat lover, she admired their Siamese, who was named Port. (Starboard had disappeared one night – no one was sure if he went overboard or simply took off overland on some private pilgrimage.) With a common bond established, our presence was tolerated. Deep down, Duck was a nice guy. His wife, Gaye, was a gregarious and friendly artist, more than making up for Duck's hesitant acceptance of our proximity. In some ways, it was high-density living, with the boats only separated by a small width of dock, and we were young and maybe noisy neighbours.

At the end of the main wharf there was a scruffy, soot-coated old timber yawl called *Cherie*. She had been built for the Canadian Mounted Police in the 1930s or earlier, and was flush-decked with a unique raised pilot house – unusual on a sailboat of that size and vintage. If boats could talk *Cherie* would have had many stories to tell, having seen service in the Canadian arctic. She was at the time owned by an ancient, supposedly blind, Welsh remittance man, named Gwyn Gray Hill but known as 'Roast'.

We never found out why Roast was so called. Rumour had it that due to some family calamity decades before, he had been exiled from Britain to the wilds of Canada and had since been living alone aboard his vessel. Roast wasn't very social and would grump at anyone who spoke to him. However, he took a shine to Cindy, giving her the nickname Waltzing Matilda (he had a nickname for everybody). He would often come up to the side of our boat and stand silently on the pontoon, waiting to be noticed, before impatiently tap, tap, tapping on the cabin side until a cup of tea was offered. Then he would scramble over the lifelines and plonk himself down in the cockpit. He did have a dark side, though, and often would say offensive and provocative things deliberately for effect, to see how people would react.

When Cindy first started working at the charter company we had become friends with Garth Goodwin and his wife Fiona, a young couple about our age who were running the place. They were keen and experienced sailors, Garth from South

Africa and Fi a Canadian. It was easy to relate to them, having similar interests and being at a parallel phase of life. Later in the summer Garth's father, John, who was world cruising aboard his yacht *Speedwell of Good Hope*, made a mammoth non-stop passage from Panama to British Columbia to come and spend some time with Garth and Fi.

I had been looking forward to meeting John, as I was familiar with his reputation as a 'single-hander'. I knew that he had made an exceptionally efficient transatlantic voyage in the 1950s (when everything was much harder) in a Laurent Giles-designed Vertue – a lovely sloop the same length as *Deus Regit II*. I had long admired the design and had read about his solo passage on *Speedwell of Hong Kong* from Barbados to Cape Town; at the time it was a bit of a record. I was always fascinated to meet these older sailors, true adventurers – pioneers, really – who set standards for seamanship and often developed new techniques in long-distance cruising.

John and his Swedish partner, Gudrun, arrived in BC and came to live on the dock adjacent to us at Cove Yachts aboard the new 48-foot *Speedwell*, so we were able to get to know them. Gudrun and Cindy got on well and developed a close friendship. The much larger *Speedwell* had the main living area in the sumptuous

Snow one cold morning in Maple Bay – it never matters how cold it gets with Cindy's smile and attitude to warm the heart

aft cabin, with the galley and large U-shaped sofa and dinette across the width of the space. It was a welcoming place to visit, especially in winter, with a wood-burning stove that provided cosy warmth. On our boat, with our uninsulated fibreglass hull and a shore-power electric heater running full-time, we could only get the interior to 9 or 10 degrees Celsius!

About half way through our year-long work visas, we discovered Cindy was pregnant. This was a curve ball we hadn't expected! We were delighted, but hadn't planned on having a baby at this stage and we were probably a bit casual about the pregnancy.

Among other things, we had to reconsider our plan to cruise to Alaska the next summer, as we had hoped to do when our work permits expired. We decided it would be best to stay in Maple Bay (pending visa extensions), where we had a great network of friends, good jobs, and had become involved with a local church.

XI

New Crew and Departure to the South

S TAYING IN MAPLE BAY proved to be a good decision. We received excellent health care from a doctor who had taken Cindy under her wing after some early complications with the pregnancy: during a routine check-up Cindy was rushed to hospital and it looked like we might lose our unexpected miracle. We suddenly realised what an amazing process we were involved in, and how devastating a loss would be. On the advice of this doctor, herself a seasoned cruising sailor, Cindy gave up her work and settled down to rest as the pregnancy continued on track. The doctor kept a close eye on Cindy throughout her pregnancy.

When old Roast found out that Cindy was having a baby, he made no bones about suggesting that she should find a way to get rid of it, because there were already enough people in the world and there was no room for yet another 'spratling'. He maintained this stance vigorously until he heard about the complications that landed Cindy in hospital.

Roast was quite distressed by this news. He hovered nearby as I worked under a yacht on the hard stand and wanted to know how Waltzing Matilda was getting on, and if 'the little kangaroo' was alright. He was genuinely concerned for her, and from then on was very polite to Cindy. After Annie was born he would still check in for his cup of tea, asking how the little Squeaker was settling in (establishing yet another nickname).

With the baby due three months after our work permits expired, we needed to figure out how to stay longer in BC. We made contact with the Canadian Consul in the USA, regarding extending our 'one-off work permits'. As it happened, the day we phoned our contact down in Seattle she was meeting with the consul in charge, and he was about to leave for a holiday in the Caribbean – coincidentally, on a charter sailing trip. Our story caught his imagination and, amazingly, he gave us the green light for the extension over the phone!

We still had to process the paperwork from outside of Canada, which meant a trip to Seattle for meetings and the application. This was a good excuse to go for a sail, and we cruised in company with our good friends Frank and Jenny Davis, a retired couple we'd met at Bible school. We had spent many good times together in their lovely waterfront home near Ladysmith. They were much older than our parents, but hanging out with Frank made me feel like the old one – he had so much energy and enthusiasm and was always developing some new idea in his basement workshop. Jenny was his biggest fan, and loved and accepted everyone around her. We would often drive up unannounced, but Frank and Jenny always had time for us, not to mention an endless supply of fresh muffins and baked goods that Jenny kept on hand for unexpected visitors.

Frank and Jenny had recently restored a sailboat similar in size to ours, and were keen to try her out. I think Jenny was also determined to keep an eye on Cindy to make sure that she wasn't overdoing it. We cruised down to Seattle, in Puget Sound, via the San Juan Islands and Port Townsend, making the round trip over a two-week period and enjoying being off the dock for a change. The countless islands and sheltered bays in which to anchor make sailing the inland waterways of the Pacific Northwest and British Columbia truly great fun. There is a remarkable absence of swell among the islands – except on a heavy-air day when a vicious chop can build, especially in wind-against-tide scenarios. But even on those days it was easy to find a secure haven and hang out for more suitable conditions. Having the luxury of time, we sailed with Jenny and Frank to a nice, relaxed schedule.

Our visas were expedited and available soon after we returned to Canada. While we continued to enjoy Maple Bay as a base, we were also preparing for the arrival of the baby and thinking about our impending departure in the fall. After two freezing winters in Canada – when the water around *Deus Regit II* iced up and condensation in lockers inside the boat actually froze – we were looking forward to warmer weather and to exploring new cruising grounds at a more leisurely pace than on our outward trip from Australia. We had a loose plan to head south to Mexico via San Francisco.

We were expecting the baby in mid-August, and our visas ended the first week of September – so it seemed as though events were on a converging course. I don't think we had any real concerns about having a baby move in with us; we had met other families who cruised with kids without any major problems, and we enjoyed a healthy lifestyle and simply expected that our kids would thrive.

As the big day drew closer, some friends expressed concern at our plans to continue ocean cruising once the baby had arrived – they were probably hoping we would settle down. But by then living aboard was natural to us, and we didn't share their concerns.

One day in August I was working on a rigging job in the boatyard, while Cindy had gone to town for a routine visit to the doctor and lunch with her friend Brenda. However, I suddenly received a call from Cindy saying that the doctor wanted her in hospital right then and there, and that the baby would need to be induced – whatever that was…

Although Cindy assured me that it would all take time, and that I should continue working for a while, my brain went to mush and I had difficulty focusing. I told Phil that I couldn't hang around; he knew where I was coming from and, grinning, wished me luck. I took off to see how Cindy was doing, which made me feel better, but I am not sure how helpful I was.

It was Friday, 18 August 1989, and by 8 pm that night we were the proud (and exhausted) parents of a beautiful daughter, Annie. The birth went well and we actually had a fun, though hard-working, afternoon. Brenda and her husband, Ken, spent the day with us, cheering Cindy on. They are a lively couple, and we all laughed a lot. They stayed until the final moments when hospital staff kicked them out to wait in the corridor.

After five days in hospital, Cindy and Annie were ready to move back on

Cindy and Annie move back on board on Day 5

Proud parents – home onboard in Maple Bay with Annie at 5 days

board *Deus Regit II*. Some of Cindy's work colleagues had given her a woven cane baby basket as a gift, and it fit perfectly in the quarter berth, making a safe, cosy little bunk for Annie, who settled in right away, sleeping like the proverbial baby, 12 hours through the night. She didn't give us any trouble – we thought it was all pretty normal; apparently babies find the constant gentle motion of a boat, even in still water, soothing. So the settling-in part was easy for all of us.

Meanwhile, temperatures were cooling and the leaves were starting to change colour, heralding the change of season. We began preparations for the trip south. So as not to wear out the girls after their recent transition, we decided that Cindy and Annie should skip the first offshore leg and travel overland, stopping off with friends in Oregon. I would sail solo to San Francisco, the first stop on our itinerary, and once in California I could rent a car and drive up to collect them. We would make the short sail together to the USA across the straits, and the girls could catch the bus down from Washington State.

With our little girl less than three weeks old, I put in my notice at Cove Yachts, announcing we'd be leaving at the end of the week. This surprised our friends, who had forgotten that we would be taking off so soon.

On 8 September at 7 pm, enjoying the slow fall twilight and with many friends and the crew from Cove Yachts waving us off, we said farewell to Maple Bay after a stay of almost 16 months. Motoring a short distance to a wharf where Jenny and Frank were staying – helping out at a summer camp – we did a brief touch and go, saying goodbye. Jenny was crying, and we felt terrible knowing how concerned she was about us setting sail with Annie, her adopted granddaughter, so soon. We passed the keys to our old Toyota to Frank, hoping that he might be able to sell it and send us some money down the track.

We were finally on our way. Only a mile or two from Maple Bay we ran into some other friends on a 50-footer named *Astrocyte*. They were arriving back from circumnavigating Vancouver Island and turned about to follow us for a while, chatting across the water. They ended up accompanying us about 6 miles to Musgrave's Landing, on Saltspring Island, where we shared a meal on board, hearing stories of their recent trip, and we enjoyed our first night away, berthed alongside the public dock.

Leaving Musgrave's the following morning, we enjoyed a fast run down the narrows between islands. Later, the wind headed us, causing us to beat to windward. I must have been a bit gung-ho, and even a little rusty, as during a gust the boat heeled suddenly, creating some tension for Cindy and Annie down below. I had to back right off until we had all settled in. We motor-sailed for a while, until we had a better wind angle to sail more comfortably.

We headed directly towards Friday Harbor in the San Juan Islands, where we were set to clear into the USA and visit John and Eileen, a friendly older couple we had met on board their boat *Jolina* in Hilo, Hawaii, two years before. It was nice to see them, and they seemed pleased at how we had changed and grown as a family, and how *Deus Regit II* – with her new gear and modifications – looked better equipped and more seaworthy.

We could have stayed for weeks visiting and cruising this area – there were so many islands and small villages to explore. However, we were on a bit of a mission to keep moving: the temperature dropped further every day and the weather would be changing soon. We needed to make this first major passage during the milder fall weather, so we set out again after only a couple of days.

From Friday Harbor we sailed almost 40 miles towards Port Townsend via Cattle Pass, enjoying the opportunity to test the new spinnaker we had picked up second-hand during the summer. A little further south we called in at Hadlock to visit Paul and Andrea Zeusche. They had built *Antalya*, a beautiful 47-foot wooden Colin Archer design, in New Zealand, then cruised for several years, ending up in the USA. Arriving in the evening we rafted up to *Antalya*, with *Deus Regit II* looking like a tender alongside. Later we moved off and anchored close by.

From Port Townsend we made arrangements for the girls to travel overland to Eugene, Oregon, to stay with friends, Jamie and Ilene Pyles and their family. It was weird seeing Cindy off with the baby; six hours alone on a bus seemed like a big deal and a long way to travel. We'd also heard negative stories of bus travel in the States and friends thought it was a bad idea, so we were a bit stressed. Our limited budget dictated the decision, but with hindsight, for the sake of $100, I probably should have rented a car and enjoyed two days driving the round trip!

Once Cindy and Annie were on the road, I took care of a few things before my planned move to Port Townsend the next day, including double-checking the tide charts to optimise my transit down the Strait of Juan de Fuca. I was looking forward to sailing again. That night I spoke with Cindy by phone, confirming that she and Annie had made it safely to Eugene, and I went to bed feeling more relaxed and ready for departure the following day.

XII

Solo

I N THE MORNING I sailed from Hadlock up to Port Townsend to take on fuel and water. Leaving the boat at the dock, I took a short walk about town and sent Cindy a note from the post office, care of our friends' address in Oregon.

Needing to wait to take advantage of a favourable tide to get me started, I sailed a few miles past Port Townsend and picked up a mooring behind a headland at the entrance of the straits, using the time there to prepare a meal and make a thermos of coffee for the long night ahead. The first seventy to eighty miles were going to be the hardest. There was much shipping traffic in the Juan de Fuca Strait, and even though I would stay outside the shipping lanes and closer to shore I would still need to be vigilant as I headed west towards Cape Flattery and the open sea.

At 5 p.m. on Wednesday, 13 September 1989, I dropped the mooring behind Point Wilson and headed off. It was glassy calm as I made my way along the shoreline, motoring quietly to maintain schedule and keep up with the tide. Before long, after some hand-bearing plots, I calculated that the tidal flow was giving me a lift of about three knots. The only trouble with a favourable current is that at some point it will become unfavourable, and I wanted to use this helpful stream for as long as possible before it changed.

I wasn't expecting to motor for long, but the wind was gone. In the early evening light, I passed a 34-footer named *Together* which was heading in the other direction, and we spoke briefly on the VHF radio (installed recently at Maple Bay).

I was in a mellow, reflective mood, watching the lights of Victoria BC fade into the distance across the Straits as the boat chugged along, rippling the mirror-like stillness of the water. I wrote up my logbook by the light of the almost-full moon. Cindy and I had good memories of our time in Canada. We were leaving just two weeks short of two years and, even though it had always been the plan, I found it hard to believe that we were actually moving on. I was at once sad and excited, and grateful that we'd had the opportunity to spend part of our lives there.

It was the first place we had lived together for any length of time, and it felt like we were leaving home. It had been a privilege and we carried with us a pretty major Canadian souvenir in the form of Annie.

Looking ahead, I decided to take advantage of the proximity of a small harbour to stop and replace the petrol I had used so far, ensuring that I had enough for the night if the lack of wind continued. To be honest, I was happy to motor-sail in the gentle conditions. Remembering how hard it had blown from the west in the Juan de Fuca Strait when we had first arrived from Hawaii, I didn't fancy a hard beat to windward in confined coastal waters for the beginning of my first major solo outing.

It was about 11 p.m. when I landed on the first vacant dock I came to in Port Angeles and went ashore to look for an open gas station. At the wharf, an old guy working on his fishing boat spotted the jerry cans I was carrying and volunteered the use of his pickup truck! Handing me a set of keys, he directed me to the local 24-hour gas station, mentioning the brand of his favourite beer.

Within an hour, with tanks full, I was back outside the harbour entrance and chugging away, almost without missing a beat. I marvelled at how welcoming and trusting strangers can be, and at how the fisherman's schedule had tied in with mine that night.

It was a pleasant, relatively uneventful night – a nice thing to be able to say about any passage! The following morning, at around 10 a.m., I entered Neah Bay for the second time (we had stopped here briefly on our way north two years earlier). Not a lot had changed in this small, isolated fishing village, perched at the edge of the Olympic Peninsula within 6 miles of Cape Flattery, the north-western-most point of the contiguous United States. The town could be best described as rustic, with rough docks and timber decking covered in sea bird droppings.

I spent only a few hours there, eating lunch at a diner that was almost as rustic as the marina and topping up my tanks again, having motored in zero wind for the entire 17-hour passage. As I sailed out, just off the harbour entrance I spotted a familiar yellow cutter heading into Neah Bay, and we both altered course towards each other at about the same time. It was *Pegasus*, a Westsail 32, with her American owner Rod Thompson on board.

Rod was also single-handing. We'd become friendly in Maple Bay, as he had his boat hauled and maintained there during the last two seasons. I was happy to see a familiar face, and we chatted briefly and then waved each other on. Even though Rod was leaving the next day and heading in the same direction as me, it would be almost 18 months before our paths would cross again, thousands of miles away in southern Mexico.

From Cape Flattery to San Francisco is 650 nautical miles, and my route would take me down the Washington, Oregon, and California coastlines. The area had a fearsome reputation in the eyes of the Canadian and Pacific Northwest sailors, who are used to sailing among islands and inlets surrounded by high land. Usually this was their first taste of offshore experience.

There are limited places to stop off easily, as most of the rivers are barred and can be quite dangerous. Constant big swells and weather coming from the west create a lee shore. These factors are intensified when gales blow in, making for a challenging leg even for experienced sailors – it's advisable to keep a good distance offshore.

My passage plan was simple: I needed to angle away from the coast, taking *Deus Regit II* well offshore, then head directly south, keeping about 40–50 nautical miles clear of the major headlands of Cabo Blanco and Cape Mendocino. Once at 40 degrees north latitude, I could start to head inshore again to close the coast near Point Reyes, where I would make landfall, before completing the final 40 miles in to the Golden Gate at the entrance to San Francisco Bay.

Being outside the straits in the rolling ocean swell for the first time in two years felt new and interesting. There was still little wind, and *Deus Regit II* was thrown about in the big, lumpy groundswell. Combined with the stress of leaving Cindy and Annie for the first time, and this being my first solo passage of significance, the trip ahead loomed a little larger than I expected.

Usually, any pre-departure nerves would subside once I cast off the lines and got underway. But this time I felt unsettled, with conflicting thoughts and new emotions swirling inside me. I had left Cindy and Annie to fend for themselves with very little money in a foreign country; what if something should happen to me, with no backup plan? Was I being irresponsible and selfish?

Some time before, when we had mentioned to friends that I would do this leg solo, John from *Speedwell* had taken me aside and given me a dressing down, saying that I was being reckless and that single-handing was not a sensible option or even considerate. "It can be tough, and technically impossible to keep a proper look out", he said, recommending that I should take on a crew. I respected John and his opinion, so I was bothered by that conversation. But ironically he had made significant passages on his own, and I thought he might understand why I wanted to take on the challenge.

The real reason I was determined to go solo was that I had always wanted and planned to be a single-hander, and this leg offered me the opportunity to take my experience to the next level. I had also been contemplating another idea for a while and had broached the subject with Cindy, but first I needed to do some research and see how I fared on my own.

The good thing about making a passage at sea is that life gets pared down to basic principles, and you don't really have time for second thoughts. The job description is pretty straightforward: keep the boat moving, sail sensibly, don't drop the ball in regards to navigation, and keep the boat in good shape and the crew healthy.

When circumstances seem bigger than they are, and we are being stretched personally and sometimes physically, it's an opportunity to reflect on who you believe is in control. My conviction is that God has our best interests at heart, giving us choices and challenges in life; the challenges often provide clarity, so we can see how good and reliable He is. Remembering it wasn't all up to me, I was able to refocus on the task at hand and soon started to relax and unwind. With still no wind, and the poor boat rolling about in a big greasy swell, I started the outboard and began to chug away on an offshore slant at about four knots. At least with the mainsail up and a bit of way on, the boat wasn't being buffeted so much and the uncomfortable motion settled – as did my stomach!

Even though I felt conflicting emotions as I set out on the passage, it was something I had been looking forward to all my life. My childhood goal of sailing solo around the world, still embedded deep within my psyche, had resurfaced earlier that year.

It was the middle of winter and we had been invited to a friend's yacht one evening. After dinner we watched videos of the 1982 and 1986 editions of the BOC Challenge single-handed round-the-world race. For me it was an intensely exciting night! I remember leaving the wood-fired warmth of Hap and Carlita's 50-footer and walking with Cindy through the snow across the dock to our little boat; and a conviction took hold in my gut that this might be the format for me to pursue the ambition of a solo circumnavigation that I had kept close since I was a boy.

Not long after, Thom Reidl gave me a copy of a book written by Canadian

John Hughes about his experience sailing in the 1986 BOC Challenge; this added fuel to the fire, helping me form a rudimentary plan.

Growing up, I was inspired by the likes of Robin Lee Graham, who sailed around the world in the 24-foot *Dove* as a teenager. Bernard Moitessier, a French single-hander, had the gift of being able to brilliantly communicate the allure of the sea, its romance and purity, as well as the harshness of the environment and the raw power of an indiscriminate ocean. His books offered pragmatic advice, pertinent to exemplary seamanship, and demonstrated the persistence needed for successful long-distance voyaging, which for him was the ultimate form of self-expression.

I absorbed accounts of many other early single-handers: Harry Pigeon, Alain Gerbault, Robin Knox-Johnston, David Lewis, John Guzzwell in the tiny *Trekka*, and of course Joshua Slocum, who headed off in 1895 on a three-year voyage and became the first person to make a solo circumnavigation under sail.

When I was in school, a few of my teachers realised that I had little interest in the usual curriculum; so they stocked the library with books on navigation, sailing, and yacht design. Most were technically above my pay grade as a 12 and 13-year-old, but I read them anyway. I am sure my name was the only one ever registered on the borrowed tab of the library card.

These deep desires and motivations take us places in life, as we respond to opportunities along the way. I feel that my desire to sail was inherent in my character and part of the process that shaped me as an individual.

Well, here I was – certainly an individual and definitely 'out there', with the opportunity to see for myself if I was up to the challenge.

With evening came a light breeze from the north. It wasn't much, but it allowed me to shut off the motor and begin to sail. The light conditions remained for the next few days – I was wondering why I had been so stressed! I would have liked to have been sailing faster, but was glad the area wasn't living up to its usual nasty reputation.

That first night's run was dismal: when I worked up my dead reckoning 19 hours after departing Cape Flattery I found we had covered only about 52 nautical miles. It had been a tricky night. I was trying to re-establish an unfamiliar routine, and the swell remained high and winds light – a combination that can be uncomfortable, to say the least.

Importantly, I was no longer using the sheet-to-tiller method for self-steering. We had installed a wind-vane self-steering device that was custom made in Massachusetts, on the East Coast of the States, by an engineer named Gerard Ratcliffe. It was a development of the servo-pendulum vane gears like the Aries or Monitor types, but was much smaller and more compact, suiting our small boat better for weight and, of course, aesthetics.

The polished stainless steel, with artful bearings and linkages, was attractive, but more importantly it was robust and worked perfectly. We had tested it out on day sails in the waters near Maple Bay, but being on the open ocean again it felt wonderful to see the vane kick in and take charge. In the fickle, rolling conditions it took some initial tweaking to get it up and running, but once set, 'Ratso' – the nickname by which we referred to the vane gear – took firm control and steered beautifully, responding to each shift of the breeze.

This really was progress. We were fortunate that *Deus Regit II* had such good inherent directional stability, which had allowed us to adopt the sheet-to-tiller method so successfully on the way over. However, with the reliability of the new wind vane and the power that it generated, I was able to focus on sailing the boat and trimming the sails for best speed; everything was working for maximum benefit without having to compromise trim and speed for the sake of freedom from the need to hand steer.

The light winds continued till the third day out, when I finally broke through the three-knot barrier and had a day's run in excess of a hundred miles – my daily target. We topped out at 108 nautical miles between noon fixes.

One time, as I was reefing the main and still clambering about on deck finding my sea legs, my wedding ring suddenly slipped off my cold, damp finger. I heard, rather than saw, the ring hit the deck, and I froze. Remarkably, it didn't bounce off the narrow side-deck into the sea, but remained on edge, spinning like a top. I pounced on it, shoving it back on my finger with relief, and returned to finish tying in the reef pennants.

The steady if unremarkable progress continued, with winds building to around 20 knots, varying in direction from the north-east to the north-west and gusting quite strongly. I had to gybe occasionally in squalls, with grey scudding clouds. The wind picked up on the fourth night so that I was running with just a portion of the partly rolled genoa out, flying and making excellent time.

I was thrilled to be making a foray into the solo sailing scene, but I was starting to feel that the ambition of the single-handed race around the world might be too much for me. It started to seem a bit silly, and perhaps selfish, to deliberately leave Cindy and our new daughter behind for an adventure. I was torn, thinking I should quit while I was ahead, and maybe put the notion behind me once I had this small passage safely out of the way.

The helpful brisk winds eased off, and we were under full sail again in favourable, lighter, though patchy, conditions. However, my patience was tested when we made a 24-hour run of only 78 miles.

That afternoon I was down below when I heard an incredibly loud roar. Tearing outside, at first I could see nothing obvious nearby, but then I spotted a small military jet – a dot in the sky about a mile away. Making a turn, it came barrelling towards me again, screaming overhead at what appeared to be just above mast height, and then belted off into the grey cloud towards the coast. This jet incident must have been inspirational, because by the next day we had made an incredible 154 miles on track – the best day's run since leaving Australia. It showed how effective the new vane gear was when everything was in the groove. However it was a fluky weather pattern I was sailing in, as the very next day we made only 43 miles.

I lacked confidence in that day's noon fix, and tried several times during the afternoon to get confirmation with another position line to cross with my earlier efforts. (I had made a mistake converting LHA.) I had been at sea for one week, and was at the limit where I needed to alter course to close with the coast for my approach to San Francisco.

Though these secondary plots in the afternoon didn't confirm or deny my accuracy, I made a course change heading for the coast so that at least if the navigation was out I could get my bearings with a sight of land. I was thinking that a ship would be good thing to see, and possibly ask for a fix, so that I wasn't making landfall blind. Little did I know how blind I would be.

It was important not to end up south of San Francisco's latitude, as it would mean beating back against the wind and seas that had been so helpful to me on this leg. Going the other way – upwind – would be a different matter. Around 8 p.m. I spotted another vessel's navigation lights and hailed them on VHF radio. I had seen a large sail boat and identified myself as the small yacht on their starboard side, hoping that they might see my torch-lit sails nearby. After repeated calls with no reply, I started to feel frustrated, wondering why they wouldn't answer their radio. I could hear radio chatter from a shore station in San Francisco and other vessels, and felt that my installation was functioning okay.

It was an exasperating hour for me, with sheets hardened in, close-hauled, to gain some with the larger yacht. It was peculiar that they were travelling so slowly, just milling about, coming in from further seaward and north of me. I assumed that my fresh wind at 20 knots was less effective for the big, heavy cruising ketch, so that they were only jogging along. Eventually they spoke on the VHF and turned a few degrees in my direction.

When I drew close enough to recognise details of the boat, I was bewildered to discover that it was a 65-footer I had painted the previous two seasons at Cove Yachts. I told them who I was, but they still showed no interest, nor did they respond to my request for their position until I was close enough to see the crew standing in the pilot house. In the end, they reluctantly gave me their latitude and longitude, confirming my own sun-sights from earlier in the day when I had made an error. I hadn't been convinced by my reworked calculations, but now I found that all the effort I had put in to communicate with the cagey boat was a little redundant.

The confirmation of my position showed that I was on course, with only eighty miles to sail. If I had just enjoyed a meal and the sunset, trusting my own abilities, my life would have been easier! It reconfirmed what I already knew: you really are out there on your own, and it was my responsibility to know where I was, and where I was going.

As I resumed my course, the other boat appeared to linger where they were, and I didn't see them again. In hindsight, I wondered what they were up to out there...

An hour later I was sailing in dense fog and was very glad to have been able to double-check my position. I enjoyed terrific reaching winds all night, and *Deus Regit II* had a bone in her teeth with the prospect of another landfall as we sailed at a steady 5–6-knot average.

The fog persisted all night, and I again experienced the ethereal sensation of sailing in a fragile bubble. We made our way towards the coast, about to enter some major shipping lanes on the approach to this major port city, San Francisco. Between catnaps I kept a diligent watch that night – not so much for shipping, as visibility of 200 metres made that almost a moot point; rather, I kept an eye on our heading and speed so that the dead-reckoning log would be as sharp as possible. I made an allowance for set and drift and plotted this on the chart hourly.

At 7 a.m. I popped my head up from a nap and was surprised to see, close on my port side, another sail boat. It was a schooner, I think from British Columbia, and I wished them good morning on VHF. Ken, the owner of *Tethys*, was friendly

– the opposite of whoever grudgingly spoke with me the night before on the other boat. He volunteered a satnav position and I was encouraged when it tied well with my DR plots, confirming that we had 24.8 miles left to run. I felt blessed by the timing of our meeting; it certainly took some pressure off in that fog.

For the remainder of the run in we sailed in sight of each other – and I appreciated having someone nearby in the limited visibility. Occasionally I heard sound signals from shipping moving in the blanket of fog; once I was startled as the profile of a large merchant vessel emerged from the mist close beside me, running a parallel course and disappearing ahead moments later.

Four more hours and our progress had slowed a little, but *Deus Regit II* kept sailing nicely and I was delighted to have made the passage in good time. The modifications and equipment we had installed in BC had worked well in the real world of ocean sailing; the windvane was worth its weight in gold, with its sure and powerfully sensitive steering. The skipper perhaps needed to work on his confidence, but he was keen to keep on learning.

Near noon, land to the north vaguely emerged into view through the haze, and within a few minutes we had sailed out of the foggy bubble. There, right on course and clear as day about five miles away, were the red spans of the Golden Gate Bridge. The flood tide was set to run for the rest of the afternoon and would ease our entry.

The Golden Gate Bridge had only an hour before been ensconced in fog as Deus Regit II *sailed in – a nice end to a challenging passage down from Canada*

I was elated. Sailing under the monumental Golden Gate Bridge was a memorable moment and held special significance for me: passing beneath such a famous landmark was in itself an important milestone, especially at the end of a challenging passage; and San Francisco was also the home port of our very good friends Stephen and Marja Vance, whom I had met as a teenager sailing in New Zealand almost ten years before. At that time they had been part way through what would become a seven-year circumnavigation in their yacht *Twiga*, a Cal 2-27.

Over the years, Steve and Marja have played a big part in my life and that of my family. When we first met, an easy friendship formed, developing over time to that of an adopted family. They always encouraged my youthful enthusiasm and interest in yachting and the voyaging lifestyle. They mentored me about seamanship and sailing, as well as imparting some positive wisdom when, at 17, I was independent of my parents but still a kid needing some direction.

Sailing my own boat to rendezvous with them aboard *Twiga* was a kind of homecoming, and I was looking forward to introducing them to Cindy and, of course, our new crew, Annie.

I spoke to *Tethys* on the VHF one last time as they made their way into a marina just past the entrance to the Gate. Meanwhile, I headed over to the eastern side of San Francisco Bay and up the Alameda estuary, sharing the channel with container ships using the terminal at Oakland. My destination was Marina Village, where Marja worked as the marina manager. She had reserved a slip for me and I was excited to call her at the office on the VHF radio.

Following Marja's instructions, I sailed *Deus Regit II* into a berth alongside *Twiga*, completing the eight-day leg from Canada. Marja welcomed me warmly; we were delighted to see each other after a gap of several years, picking up our friendship without missing a beat. I would catch up with Stephen in a few days' time, when he returned from working in Alaska.

XIII

The Bay Area

THE DAY AFTER ARRIVING in San Fancisco, I rented a car and headed off on the almost 1800-kilometre (1100-mile) round trip to Oregon to collect the girls from our friends' place near Eugene. The contrast between sea and road travel was disconcerting. Suddenly I was barrelling down the highway at high speed, covering distances in one or two hours that had just taken me a day or two under sail. It seemed absurd. I was relieved and happy after a few days to be back home on *Deus Regit II*, together with my family.

We enjoyed reconnecting with old friends in Alameda, among them Jim and Ann Cate on *Insatiable*, whom we had met in Hawaii two years before. They had sailed back to San Francisco and were living at Marina Village, preparing their 36-footer to set sail again the following season, like many other cruisers living aboard in the marina.

Owning a boat means there is always a project needing attention. Being back on a convenient dock allowed me much-needed time to catch up with a few jobs without the rush of our recent Maple Bay departure. We fitted a large 80-watt solar panel on a swivelling, tilting bracket – easily adjustable to capture the sun at various angles – which would abundantly serve our meagre 12-volt power needs.

Cindy was still recovering from the birth, and we planned to remain for several weeks to relax, let Annie grow a bit, and arrange for her immunisations and other infant care while good health services were nearby.

With Steve back from Alaska, the following week we embarked on a trip up the Sacramento Delta, with Steve and Marja on *Twiga*, and some Canadian friends who had arrived in Alameda in time to join us on their 28-foot Bristol Channel Cutter, *Tremil Sea*.

The delta is a network of rivers, cuts and channels that make up hundreds of miles of inland waterways. Much of it is reclaimed swamplands, originally developed in the 1800s when a series of levees were built and the area in between was drained to create farmland tracts. It was a huge initiative, and created navigable channels for moving equipment and people by boat and barge to and from the goldfields during the great rush of 1847.

Crossing the bay, we sailed up the Sacramento and San Joaquin Rivers. Near Benicia we sailed quietly past a ghostly collection of dozens of decommissioned US Naval vessels lying to moorings. These mothballed warships were apparently ready for action if they were needed, but many had been on standby for decades.

We anchored overnight in places with interesting names like Potato Slough, Three Mile Cut and No Name Slough, and visited the historic town of Locke, built by a group of Chinese families in the early 1900s. We anchored there for a couple of quiet days, with stern lines tied to the overhanging trees on the river bank, enjoying its ramshackle, Wild West flavour.

After a few days Steve and Marja headed back to Alameda on *Twiga* to resume their work, while we spent several more days poking around in the area and enjoying the (mostly) calm, sheltered waterway with Bruce and Louise on *Tremil Sea*.

On one occasion, it wasn't so sheltered! We were motoring along a narrow cut between levees when a large sports-fishing boat came charging around a corner at a great rate of knots, pushing tons of water, its bow wave higher than our decks. The walls of water filled the space between the boat and the embankments either side, rolling rapidly towards us. The forward hatch was wide open and, with seconds to spare, Cindy rushed below, gripping it shut with her hands as our bow was immersed in the onslaught. The beast planed past, its unconcerned sports-fisher crew on deck, intent on enjoying a day on the water, oblivious as we went under and then popped out of their wake with water cascading from our decks. So much for 'no wake' rules!

Stephen and Marja Vance – proud 'grandparents' with Annie on Twiga *at Angel Island, San Francisco, 1989*

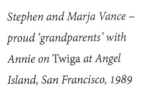

One afternoon, standing on the floating dock back at Marina Village, I was intrigued to see the deck of the pontoon begin to snake and undulate as if a huge wave had rolled into the precinct. At first I thought it was a vessel wake, but this is rare, as the large merchant ships coming into the estuary to unload at the nearby Oakland container terminal move without a ripple.

Then I noticed that the marina's concrete piles, embedded deep into the sea floor, were whipping about with increasing energy, and a vertical wave pattern coursed their length, causing the floating docks to move. Suddenly, it stopped and all was quiet. Excited people rushed about, seemingly aware of what was occurring. As I headed back to our boat to check on Cindy and Annie, I was told there had been an earthquake.

By the time I made it back, all was calm again. Smoke was rising in the direction of the city, and emergency and police vehicle sirens were wailing nearby. Seven people in the city died as a result of this magnitude 6.9 earthquake of 1989, the strongest in more than 80 years.

XIV

California Cruising

WINTER WAS CHASING US as we slid into November, and we were reminded that it was time to flee south to escape it. Reluctantly, we accelerated our plans to leave the comfort of Marina Village.

A few days after the earthquake, Cindy's sister Vanessa had flown over from New York where she was living, keen to see Cindy and of course to meet her niece. Suddenly Annie was the best dressed baby, adorned in the latest NY newborn fashion.

Vess decided to sail part way down the coast with us, probably as far as Los Angeles, so there were four of us on board as we headed away from Alameda. The boat didn't seem too crowded with three adults and a baby. By the time we left, Vess had been with us a couple of weeks. She proved to be quite flexible, and although she hadn't done much sailing she was interested to see how we had been living, and was happy to take her turn at watch keeping and be involved with the process.

We thought we might be in Mexico by Christmas, but this would depend on how the girls travelled. Annie was about 11 weeks old as we sailed under the Golden Gate, poking our nose into the Pacific swells once again. Turning south with a light, favourable breeze, we made a great start in beautiful weather, enjoying a pleasant day sail to settle everyone in. In the afternoon, we anchored at Pillar Point Harbour, about 20 miles south of the Gate. We had a comfortable first night anchored within the massive breakwater that sheltered the large, otherwise exposed bay.

San Diego was just under 500 miles south of San Francisco, and our route included rounding Point Conception, which has a fearsome reputation as 'the Cape Horn of California'. We expected that conditions might be testing; however, we sailed in favourable light-to-moderate winds from the north and north-east. We sailed slower than we'd hoped, but the easy conditions were welcome, allowing us to settle into offshore mode as our confidence grew. We made a 40-hour sail down the Big Sur coast, with its backdrop of rugged cliffs and rocky shoreline.

Cindy and I were a bit tentative: we were still getting to know Annie, and this was her introduction to ocean sailing. It was one thing to live aboard at the dock, or anchored in a sheltered waterway; now we needed to test how the realities of passage making would fit with this new family dynamic.

One afternoon, with Annie in the cockpit for a nappy change, Cindy noticed several large, dark shadows moving through the front face of the swells. Huge great white sharks were hunting sea lions. We had been wondering what was happening to the sea lions, as they were visible nearby in the swell one minute and gone the next. Now we realised that they were being snatched away by sea monsters that were as long as our boat!

As this grizzly scene played out before us, we quickly finished the task at hand and put Annie safely back in her bunk below. Cindy, Vanessa, and I watched nature at work for a while from the cockpit, tweaking as much speed out of *Deus Regit II* as we could. It was a spectacular sight, if a little unnerving.

While Cindy was on watch that night, she was reminded of our close encounter with a ship in the Juan de Fuca Strait, two years earlier. The large black shape of a freighter appeared beside her, overtaking and showing no lights. She called the phantom ship on the VHF, asking if they were aware of the yacht close on their port side. At the same time she moved our course closer to shore. With no answer from the vessel, she tried them again several times. We were all awake and in the cockpit, and once they were past us we stood there, feeling relieved and staring at the dark, disappearing silhouette of the stern of the ship. As we wondered about the obvious lack of navigation or other lights, the radio suddenly burst into life, and a deep guttural voice bellowed "We're aware!" It was a bit late, but it was all the acknowledgment we received from the ship.

Arriving in Morro Bay and creeping past the distinctive volcanic Morro Rock at the narrow harbour entrance at 3 a.m., we were able to lie along the public wharf and get some sleep.

Vanessa had fitted in well on board, untroubled by seasickness or the close confines. She was due to fly back to New York in a few days, so we explored the town together over the weekend before she took a bus to LA to catch her flight. We had enjoyed having her with us, and Cindy appreciated the family support so far from home with a new baby.

We needn't have worried about Annie adjusting to life on the boat; she set-tled in and was content hanging out with her mum and dad. Every now and then we would hear a squeak and check in with her, barely an arm's length away in her basket. She loved being outside while we sailed, held close to our chests but exposed and feeling the wind in her face. She responded with delighted clucks and gurgles and coos. We thought that this parenting thing wasn't so hard.

Rounding Point Conception unscathed one afternoon, we anchored among kelp beds for a time at Cojo Anchorage, an open roadstead. On that day, and I think most days, it was rolly and uncomfortable, so during the night we decided to abandon the awkward anchorage and sail the forty miles to Santa Barbara. To our surprise, we sailed almost immediately into dense fog. We had expected perpetual summer in the fabled Southern Californian waters: the weather certainly is milder and more temperate, but warm air rolling off the land condenses as it meets the colder waters, making fog a regular occurrence.

Annie loved being at sea

We had previously laid off a series of course lines to clear the oil rigs on our path to Santa Barbara, but as the fog enveloped us, all we could do was sail by compass and hope we could pick up the glow of light from an oil rig platform for perspective as we drifted past in light winds.

When working on the passage plan for this section I had clipped a notice from *Latitude 38* magazine with the up-to-date latitude and longitude for each of the oil platforms in the Santa Barbara channel. The platforms that concerned us were each named with an H-word, such as Hondo, Heritage, Harmony, Helen, and Herman. Leap frogging them, one rig at a time, worked well, but the glare of the work lights and fast-flashing buoy lights surrounding the mysterious-looking structures created a strange environment.

The following morning we spoke to a shrimp boat, at around 8 a.m. Calling across the water, they assured us we were on track and that Santa Barbara lay ten miles ahead in the gloom.

Santa Barbara, with its holiday atmosphere, was good to us, and we stayed three nights. The local yacht club allocated us a rare vacant berth for a night, and we made good use of the convenient laundry and shower facilities before moving to anchor outside the crowded yacht harbour by Stearns Wharf with other transient yachts. Jutting out into the bay beyond the breakwater, the wharf was originally for merchant ships to load and unload, and it had become a major attraction, populated with vendors and restaurants, where tourists could stroll and enjoy the view.

As we were preparing to move on, I went to buy petrol for the outboard. I was contemplating walking into town to get fuel from a regular gas station rather than paying the premium for filling our cans at the fuel dock. But when I asked the owner if it might be cheaper in town, he replied, "If you're on a budget, take what you need; we've had an awesome month." I thought he was having a go at me, but he was sincere! We topped up our tanks and were at capacity for the first time in a while, for which we were thankful.

Once in Southern California we started to meet other cruising yachts, most of them, like us, bound for Mexico. And for the first time, we met people our own age out sailing. Most yachties seemed to be responsible older people, who'd set sail once they'd seen off their kids and sold property or businesses, or otherwise transitioned from successful shore-based lives.

We really enjoyed meeting travellers closer to us in age. Our conversations were maybe more animated, and someone always hatched a plan to explore ashore or find the cheapest happy hour where food was included if you bought a beer or a soda. Martin Picard was the first of these younger sailors we met. He was sailing aboard *Orca*, the Hans Christian 33 he had single-handed down from San Francisco as stage one of a voyage to Europe via Australia.

Speeding up to *Deus Regit II* in his outboard-powered inflatable, Martin executed what we came to recognise as a signature move, dropping the boat off the plane to stop just a few feet short, with the boat's wake bashing into our topsides with a splash. He introduced himself, saying he had spotted our flag and was on his way to Sydney; then he asked pointedly, "Is that fresh baked cookies I can smell?", as he held onto our topsides and chatted from the tender. We invited him on board, and so started a lasting friendship.

We moved further on to Oxnard and checked in at the Channel Islands Yacht Club, where they offered us a free berth for a 'few days' which stretched to nine. We always appreciated it when yacht clubs extended us a courtesy berth. All the harbours along the California coast are artificial, dredged and cut into the surrounding land, with great stone breakwaters built up for protection. Since they have nil or limited space for boats to anchor out or lay to a swinging mooring, we were restricted to staying in these comfortable but sometimes expensive marinas. While convenient, it did impact our cruising budget.

At Oxnard we docked beside a larger sailboat whose owner jumped to the pontoon, greeting us and taking our lines. After we'd checked in with the office, our neighbour reappeared and handed me a set of car keys, saying, "I'm away for a few days, you can use my truck if you want." We hadn't even exchanged names at this point! He wandered off, leaving his boat's companionway and hatches wide open and radio blaring, returning only later in the week.

It was a little breezy as we left our berth in Channel Islands Harbour early one morning, bound for King Harbour. We had planned to sail in company with another young couple we had met a few days earlier, Tom and Thalia from Seattle, on their 36-footer *Sotto le Stelle*.

Accustomed to sticking to the plan, we headed off as scheduled at around 6 a.m., giving Tom a wave as he popped his head out of the hatch. He was still preparing to leave – or so we thought. As we set sails in the narrow channel and gybed to head out of the harbour, we took off in a wind suddenly gusting more than 30 knots – and it increased as we screamed past the breakwater. Once outside, and realising that the wind was too strong for us to turn back, we carried on under heavily reefed main and jib in 40 knots of dry, intense Santa Ana wind.

We had heard about Santa Ana's notorious gale-force winds that howl off the land, setting up a pattern that can blow for several days at a time. At least we weren't beating into it. We pressed on, hurriedly getting rid of the mainsail altogether, and reached along with just a small part of the genoa unfurled, hoping it wouldn't blow any harder. It was hectic, and we understood why Tom and Thalia hadn't rushed out after us.

Fortunately for us this Santa Ana didn't blow for days, and as we closed the southern shore of Santa Monica Bay, almost fifty miles away, the wind dropped off altogether and we drifted the last few miles. Docking at the yacht club, we found that Martin was also there on *Orca*, as was *Diomedia*, a Canadian trimaran we had also met in Santa Barbara.

Tom and Thalia arrived later, adding to our fleet-within-a-fleet; an influx of mid-to-late twenties yachties suddenly converging in the one place. Hanging out together, we enjoyed lots of meaningful and fun conversation, sharing stories about 'the meaning of life', sailing and travelling, what people had been up to BC (before cruising), and what they might do in the future.

Our cruising budget was strict, comprising all the savings we had made in Canada, with the plan to find more work along the way. Our friends were at the beginning of their voyaging experience, and while everyone was being frugal and enjoyed finding ways to save money and be efficient, their budgets were in another league compared to ours. We would have liked to work in Canada or the USA for a few extra months, but being limited by the seasons, and abiding by US visa restrictions, we planned to make a timely cruise on the US coast then find work in Mexico on American and other foreign yachts.

Among our group, we swapped tips and ideas. I was interested to see that most boats were now relying on electronic navigation aids such as satnav and radar – equipment that was rarely seen on the other side of the Pacific before we left Australia. But we were in America after all; the dollar bought more, and I think technology was generally taken up sooner by the American cruising boats we met.

In King Harbour we caught up with some surfer friends we had met in a cafe at Oxnard. We had introduced ourselves because I and one of the guys in the group were wearing T-shirts with the same logo design: some mates in Australia had been involved in setting up the local Christian Surfers network, and I was wearing an Australian Christian Surfers branded T-shirt, while the other guy was wearing a Californian edition. So we got talking, as you do, and they invited us to visit their church – Hope Chapel, in Hermosa Beach. While at King Harbour we made contact, and enjoyed their hospitality and friendship.

On our first day in King Harbour, when we were tied to the yacht club dock before going out to anchor, a fellow from San Luis Obispo struck up a conversation, eagerly asking about the fish we were catching. I had to admit to having only a rod, but no lures or other equipment on board (I am not the best fisherman). He seemed a bit sad on my behalf. An hour later he returned, handing over a brown paper bag and wishing us "bon voyage", before turning abruptly and walking back to his car. Inside the bag was a kit of tackle and fishing lures, along with basic fishing instructions! Cindy was excited, and determined that we would follow the instructions.

By the beginning of December we only had about a hundred miles to sail to San Diego. We were enjoying an easy cruising pace, day-sailing in mild conditions. We planned five more stops along this route, each a leg of between 12 and 33 miles.

Leaving our 'fleet' of younger yachties, we exchanged a loose idea of itineraries and looked forward to meeting up again further south. Arriving in a new anchorage it was always a bonus to see the familiar mast of a friend's boat, or an acquaintance from a previous anchorage. We felt part of a community as we travelled.

Compared to our relatively lone Pacific voyage in 1987, this was a friendly, social group that we enjoyed being part of. We did, however, notice a tendency for some boats to become too reliant on each other. Here, for the first time, we started to hear people speaking of their 'buddy boats'. While it's fun to see friends regularly, it was a concern that some crews would amend their schedule to wait for a particular boat to leave with them. Or worse, if a particular boat were nervous and hesitant to leave – perhaps a (moderate) weather forecast was not to their liking – they might try to keep others in port to justify their own reluctance to get underway.

One friend complained that he was being stalked by a much larger, faster yacht, whose owners would only sail when our friends were underway. The bigger boat was an ultra-light race boat, and the experienced and competent – though hesitant – skipper would rip past the more conventional 37-footer and then stop, waiting for them to catch up. While leap frogging them down the coast, the skipper of the bigger boat always made sure to arrive first into port, ensuring everyone noticed his superior performance and speed. The owner was gregarious and fun to be around, so I guess it was worth putting up with his sometimes annoying swagger.

There were not many of these fast, racy, ultra-light boats in the cruising fleet, so this one stood out, but I noted that sailing range could be extended dramatically with a more performance-orientated yacht. You could sail faster and cover greater distances, with less critical weather windows; overall it should be easier and safer. I always admired that bright blue 50-footer, and it set me to thinking again about the BOC Challenge and the possibility of one day making a solo circumnavigation.

Was it a realistic goal? The motivation wasn't a result of any latent discontent on my part; it was more about my growth as a sailor. I had foregone a traditional education in my eagerness to go to sea, and I started to think of it as a form of graduation, validating my experience and the things I'd learnt along the way. My logic was partly pragmatic, considering the race as a way that we might possibly buy into a larger yacht, extend our range, and provide a more permanent home, allowing us to cruise further with more control, comfort, and speed.

These thoughts about the solo race around the world came and went like the tide. I would recall the tension I had experienced on my solo passage down to San Francisco, how irresponsible I felt, and how I missed my family. So I would put the idea aside and carry on enjoying where we were in life. We were fortunate, and we did have the best life – why mess with that?

However, we were on a path, and over time I felt moved in a direction that made it harder to ignore the idea. Tom, on *Stelle*, had mentioned meeting Mark Schrader – who had raced in the previous BOC in 1986, and who was working as a yacht broker when Tom was buying his boat in Seattle. No direct connection to me, but it did contribute: real people did stuff like this. I started to hear snippets about the next edition of the race coming up later the following year (1990). The idea continued percolating.

San Diego was a transition point for us – the end of one era and beginning of another. On leaving there, we would enter Mexico and begin to explore not only new territory but a different culture far removed from the familiar Australian and North American ones. We looked forward to it as we began stocking up on food items – mainly canned meat and fruits that we'd heard were unavailable in Mexico. Annie's four-month vaccinations were also due, and we wanted these done before we left for the remote Baja coast, where health checks may not have been available.

Christian Bastke, one of our Bible school teachers, also lived nearby, and we enjoyed spending time with him and his family, visiting their home, and having them to dinner on board when the Southwestern Yacht Club – being over-subscribed on one of their busiest days – made room for us alongside. Our guests could visit easily, and watch from 'box seats' on board in the marina, as the annual Christmas parade of hundreds of colourfully lit yachts toured the harbour at night.

Money was becoming tight. We had been stocking up and had staples on board to last several months, so would not starve, but with all the day sailing and socialising our cash savings were dwindling. *Deus Regit II* wasn't expensive to run and we lived cheaply, but we did wonder if we would make it out of California before running out of money.

We expected to be able to live even more cheaply in Mexico, and I hoped to pick up yacht deliveries or other boat work. We didn't make a point of letting people know our financial state; our friends on other boats also lived thriftily, so

Aboard Deus Regit II *with Christian Bastke, one of our Bible School teachers, a good friend and mentor*

our situation wasn't obvious. Cindy always had baked goods to share (the oven upgrade was working a treat!) and we regularly shared a meal with the single-handed sailors and other people we met.

One night, awakened at 3:30 a.m. by a rare rain shower, I heard an unusual bump. I checked on deck and all was as it should be, but in the distance I spotted a dinghy being rowed silently by two people – odd at that late hour. Then I noticed an envelope had been dropped in the cockpit. It contained $60.00 cash and a card that read "Christmas wishes from your sailing friends." On the scale of world economies it was small, but for us it was a major input and we were very thankful. Whoever dropped off the card had wished to remain anonymous – we had our suspicions, but saw no clues as we talked to suspects over the next few days.

To enter Mexico we would need to have the correct paperwork. We had heard stories of graft and corruption, and of crews being harassed by officials in various ports. There were stories of demands for payment of fines or processing fees that were vague and inconsistent. It seemed that the local authorities made it up as they went.

I was a little nervous when I went into the Mexican consul in San Diego to apply for visas for the three of us. Typically, I needn't have worried – though of course there were numerous forms to fill out (Spanish cultures at the time seemed to thrive on multiple copies). We each needed a permit to enter and a fishing licence (I talked them out of issuing one for Annie); further, we needed a licence for the dinghy and one for the primary vessel. Each item carried a separate fee!

The only issue we had was that the clerk gave me permits for 90 days when we really needed at least six months: this would have meant sailing or travelling over-land back to the States for renewals. I had to ask for someone in authority to come out and change the papers to allow for the maximum stay. Everything worked out fine, and to my relief no one asked for a donation that I was ill-equipped to pay. Nor did we ever have a negative experience with any of the officials in any of the many Mexican ports we sailed to.

XV

Viva la Mexico

L EAVING SAN DIEGO on a grey afternoon, we drifted down the main channel out past Point Loma in light winds. We were bound for Cabo San Lucas,
where we had arranged a loose rendezvous with our friends Tom and Thalia, on
Sotto le Stelle, and where we thought we might break the trip in Bahia Magdalena
('Mag Bay'), almost 600 miles south of the border.

The sea and sky were slate grey, and we trickled along in a low, smooth swell,
entertained by US military helicopters and small ships that were setting off flares
and signals for what we assumed was a training exercise out to sea. The popular
beachside suburb of Coronado was sliding by on our beam, and ahead in the distance we could vaguely see the silhouette of a small island cluster, the Islas Los
Coronados – our first glimpse of Mexico!

The soft winds persisted, and I was still using lights on Point Loma and Coronado ashore for fixes more than six hours later. Cindy and Annie were asleep, and
I was content to drift. It was comfortable, and not a bad way to begin a passage.
At around midnight Cindy took over and I had a glorious three hours in the very
level bunk, and I think we made good about 2 miles – my log records the insightful
comment: "*Wind, none!!*"

Hours later, though the sea was the same, we felt we were in new territory:
Spanish voices dominated on the radio, and in the morning a Mexican gunboat
appeared to seaward of us and we saw sails on the horizon.

We plodded on, changing sail combinations between the spinnaker and a
poled-out headsail, along with the main, as the fickle breeze allowed. It was slow
motion, and after 24 hours we had made good only 62 miles.

I always enjoy being in the frame of mind when speed and progress don't
matter. Our concentration never lapsed, and we sailed the boat as well as we could
24 hours a day, not daring to waste or miss the benefit of a useful puff of wind
or angle contributing to our daily runs, but it is liberating to be unconstrained by
schedules. With no radio capable of range beyond line of sight, we were not under

any obligation to report in or communicate with anyone, so it was easy settling back into the first longer passage we had made in a while.

Cindy landed a large tuna – our first catch! We thought that our benefactor from San Louis Obispo, who had kindly given us the fishing gear, would have been proud. The messy job of cleaning the fish fell to me, but we were rewarded with a couple of nice fillets.

After 72 hours of mostly light winds, just before dark we could see the tops of two islands and picked up a fix by bearings on the northern parts of Isla Cedros and Islas San Benito. We decided to shorten this leg and head towards Turtle Bay (the gringo name for Bahia San Bartolome), only 60 miles further on. We could be there the following morning.

The breeze was increasing as we closed the gap between the two islands, adjusting our course towards the larger, high and steep Isla Cedros. There was plenty of sea room and it was safe enough, but with no lit navigation aids on the island, sailing down the western side felt like sailing by braille. We were aware that there can be a strong current setting towards the larger island, and with no helpful moon or shore lights for reference we ran a careful dead-reckoning plot through the night.

I must have been tired when Cindy took over at 2 a.m.: I crashed, and didn't stir for almost six hours. When the building wind headed us Cindy called to tell me she was tacking, on the final approach between the headlands at the entrance to Turtle Bay, with only a mile to go. As I had slept, blissfully unaware, she had brought us round the bottom of Cedros, altering course to close the coast and clear another smaller island, Isla Navidad, taking care of the last 25–30 miles solo. I think Cindy was disappointed she didn't quite make it to anchor before waking me! We dropped the hook among six other boats – all American – and decided that this might be a good place to spend Christmas.

After we were safely anchored, the north-east wind picked up to gale force, reminiscent of the Santa Ana conditions we experienced in California. The bay was big and open, about three miles deep by three miles wide. It was reasonably comfortable, as no big waves or chop could build in the lee of the land in front of the small village where we anchored in good holding in 18 feet of water. Though gusty, it was safe enough. We didn't bother trying to go ashore until the following afternoon, when conditions had settled down.

Turtle Bay is a small, remote fishing village with difficult, rough, road access. The village itself was less than inspirational, with its dusty roads and rough tin-roofed houses, each with the ubiquitous satellite television dish bolted to the wall or roof. The people, however, looked healthy and happy. Walking the dusty streets, I was surprised to notice that everyone's clothes were spotlessly clean (though the village was surrounded by desert and with limited water available), and most articles of clothing seemed to carry recent logos and team colours, fresh out of the USA.

Wherever we went, the Mexican people were friendly and open, especially with Annie's silvery blonde head popping out of her backpack baby-carrier. Kids and adults alike would mob her, with everyone keen to touch her hair (apparently for good luck).

Sometimes antipathy can develop when a more affluent group moves among those less well-off financially or socially. We started to notice this here. Ashore one day with John and Hal from among the boats anchored with us, one of the men gave some wrapped candy to several small boys running along beside us. The kids threw it right back, with cries of protest that they only wanted *monedas*, meaning money or coins. It was an uncomfortable moment, and we heard similar stories in other places.

It was a simple scenario to set in motion. In this case, it was probably a result of some other yachties introducing an expectation by paying young kids a dollar or two to mind their dinghy, left at the jetty during excursions ashore. Mexicans are honest, and no one was going to tamper with the yacht tenders, so it was unnecessary.

The dollar or two in tips was insignificant to the American sailors, but what this did to kids was not helpful: it led to resentment, and in our case to open hostility. One US dollar (3000 pesos) at the time could buy a lot – lunch cost less than 2000 pesos – and it was an inappropriately large tip for those little boys.

There was a friendly atmosphere among the boats in the bay. We were all enjoying exploring our first Mexican port and were excited to celebrate Christmas in such a rustic, interesting place. We were invited to share dinner on board the 38-footer *Another Day*, along with a Canadian couple from *Callaloo*. Cindy baked a dessert, and each of the other boats provided contributions to the shared 'pot luck' Christmas meal. It was a festive day in easy camaraderie with the other couples, who all doted over Annie in lieu of their own family or grandkids.

We had spent the morning relaxing in our forward bunk, opening a few pre-

sents mailed to us in San Diego by Cindy's sister, Vess, and feeling thankful to be
where we were, the three of us.

After an enjoyable week in Turtle Bay, we headed out again. As we had missed
our deadline to be in Cabo for Christmas we relaxed the schedule, making a few
shorter hops to break the trip along the Baja coast towards Cabo San Lucas. We
made two day-sails, the first of which was only 52 miles to an anchorage marked
on the chart as Bahia Asunción. We arrived in the afternoon, with plenty of daylight to find room in the lee of the headland for the night. Sharing the bay with two
other yachts, we were invited for supper on board the 46-footer *Tempest*, out of San
Diego.

Leaving the following morning, we expected an easy 25-mile day in light
south-west winds, to San Hipolito. About half way there, the wind whipped up
from 10 to 40 knots in a matter of seconds and we had to scramble, with the boat
on its ear. Cindy was down below with Annie, busy securing items, while I dumped
the main, clawing it down to the boom and making a quick lash up as the wind
veered, and we ran off with a heavily reefed genoa.

After half an hour, the mini gale moderated and blew mainly from the west.
It was still very gusty; squall lines came over us, and the wind would swing to blow
more from the south. We found anchorage off the small village of San Hipolito, in
the lee of Punta Abreojos. Abreojos means 'open your eyes', on account of the reefs
and shoals nearby. We felt exposed and vulnerable with the roaring surf beach just
behind us.

I wondered if these open roadstead anchorages were a good thing: they are
often just shallow indentations offering little real protection. If you stood on the
beach and looked out to sea, you would never consider bringing a yacht there.
Maybe a surfboard…? I considered moving on, as the winds had been, at best,
erratic all day and further wind changes could put us in danger. However, conditions soon settled down, and the anchorage turned out to be quite good. We were
surprised when every light in the village snapped off at 10 p.m. and it was pitch
black: the community generator had shut down for the night.

After a leisurely start, by mid morning we were on course for Cabo San
Lazaro, 150 miles further on, and the planned stopover in its lee at remote Bahia
Santa Maria. More settled weather provided moderate north-north-east winds,
and we made reasonable progress. Our path crossed those of migrating whales,
their spray floating on the wind.

The Baja coast is extremely remote. The villages and anchorages are isolated and hard to reach by land, with dirt tracks and rugged terrain to negotiate, and they are also separated by distance on the water. Transport and delivery of goods must have been quite difficult.

We wondered what people did for a living. Baja pangas – small, tough, open, outboard-powered boats about 25 feet long – lay on the beaches ready for transport and fishing, which most villages relied on for food and trade. In this remote environment, we were surprised to often see sails from other cruising yachts on the horizon, reminding us that we really were on a well-trodden path.

Countless yachts make the seasonal sail down the Baja coast, and there was also regular shipping traffic, from tramp coastal vessels to much larger cargo and resort-style cruise ships. We would occasionally speak to ships on the VHF and even became familiar with one operator, Jean Paul, on board the cruise ship *Jubilee*. We would speak to him several times over the next few months as the ship made its regular five-day Mexico cruise out of Long Beach, California.

Cindy spoke to a northbound cargo ship early next morning and the watch officer gave her a position check which confirmed our dead-reckoning latitude, but showed that we were a mile or two to seaward of our longitude.

Navigating along this coast, where charted aids to navigation were sparse, we often resorted to using the sextant and working up sun lines, as the charts we had of the area were of a small scale and were based on old surveys lacking detail. Staying on the rhumb line between headlands would often put us a long way offshore, so landmarks that we might see, such as a ridge or the peak of a mountain range in the distance, may not have been shown on the chart as a useful point of reference.

Most nights and early mornings I could take sights off the North Star, Polaris, and with a few calculations could work out our latitude. Often this was enough to confirm our progress; otherwise, crossing it with a sun-sight line for a running fix was always reliable.

As we made for the anchorage behind Cabo San Lazaro, in Bahia Santa Maria, it became a black, moonless night, and the wide entrance, with no shore lights, was barely discernible. We adjusted course and headed in with no reference points, except the vague dark shape of the headland, and were relieved to see the nav lights of a yacht making for the same anchorage suddenly appear a few miles ahead. It was the only clue that we were in the ball park.

We set our anchor in 26 feet of water and were pleased to find shelter out of the swell behind Monte San Lazaro (390 metres). It was New Year's Eve and we saw 1990 roll around, enjoying some of Cindy's freshly baked muffins. Annie slept, content with a few more sea miles under her belt.

Two yachts shared the bay with us – the 43-foot *Aotea*, which we had followed in the night before, and Kevin and Beth from Juneau, Alaska, on board *Achates*, their Valiant 40. They paddled by in their inflatable to pass on a message they had received over the ham radio from our friends Tom and Thalia. They were already in Cabo San Lucas, ahead of us, and had been looking out for news of us.

The anchorage was fine, but the steeply shelving beach landing, with a rolling surf, was too much for the small plywood tender I had made in Canada. We were therefore confined to the boat for a few days, before sailing just 20 miles further into Bahia Magdalena.

Mag Bay is more enclosed than San Lazaro but still has issues regarding shelter, being quite open to the northerly winds that were blowing. But as there was no shore break, we managed to land and enjoy walks ashore. We also met some local fishermen living in shacks along the beach. Some lobster fishermen zoomed up to us in their panga – they loved to travel as fast as possible! – and traded a freshly caught lobster for a peaked cap. Later, on the beach, we befriended a local called Antonio, who was happy to trade us a huge bowl of shrimp for some of Cindy's cookies and a can of plums.

With a seafood selection on the menu, we tentatively set about dealing with the lobster. Our first experience with a live crustacean was in Canada, when we had caught a big mud crab. It had leapt out of the pot on the stove – as one might when sat on something hot! The lid crashed to the floor, and the crab scrabbled about on the counter top and dropped to the cabin sole before we were able to contain its lack of compliance. It was terrifying. We took this one on a little more thoughtfully, holding the lid on for a while...

Overnight, we experienced what felt at the time like a major disaster: a mesh bag of cloth nappies that had been tied alongside, soaking, came adrift, and we lost them all. We were left with only a few clean spares, which at Annie's rate of use was definitely not enough! I went in search of them to no avail, even asking our fisher friend if he had any *pañales* left from when his family were last visiting. We communicated in very poor Spanglish, and Antonio thought it was a great joke that we had lost all of our "diapers *para la niña*".

We still had more than 160 miles to sail to Cabo San Lucas – only a couple of weeks behind schedule – and it was to be our official port of entry into Mexico. We had stopped off in small, out-of-the way places, so had yet to clear customs (*aduana*) or immigration (*inmigración*).

The passage from Magdalena Bay to Los Cabos, which lay to our south-east, was interesting, to say the least. Leaving in a moderate and favourable north-east wind, we later lay becalmed for several hours, patiently waiting for a new breeze. When it came, we sailed fast and easy until late afternoon, before the wind suddenly shifted to blow hard from the south-east – exactly the direction we needed to go!

The heavy wind forced us south and to seaward of the rhumb line. Eventually the wind backed enough to allow us to lay our course, hard on the wind on port tack, clawing for any progress. Gradually the wind angle opened up and we could ease the sheets a little and sail easier. We thought we would be okay with the tougher but doable conditions, but by midnight we had stripped off the mainsail and were close-reaching in building winds of 35–40 knots. The direction was almost reasonable, but the wind had whipped up a rough sea and we were bounced around harshly. It was not a great night, both of us having forgotten what it was like to be in a real gale at sea.

The fierce wind continued through the night, setting us outside our course line and forcing us to work hard to mitigate the set and drift in the rough conditions. The next morning we crossed a line into the wind shadow of the high land, and the gale suddenly stopped; in an instant we lay becalmed again!

We hadn't taken on any fuel since leaving California. Checking what remained on board, I calculated that we had enough to motor 20 miles – but we still had 30 to go. We puttered along, alternately running the motor and drifting for most of the afternoon. With only 11 miles to go, the fuel tank ran dry. It was a shame our earlier fuel estimates had been so accurate.

But what a beautiful evening! Stars lay reflected in the water, and it was considerably warmer than the previous day. With our destination almost within reach, around the corner of Cabo Falso, and with both of us tired from the rough conditions of the last couple of days, I found it frustrating to have to break out the oars.

In Canada I had procured an old cedar oar from the rafters in Phil's shed at Cove Yachts, giving it a new lease of life with a coat of paint. In the spirit of the Pardeys (a couple who cruised the world in engineless boats for 40 years), I had stowed it on board *Deus Regit II*, lashed to the lifelines, ready for just such an occasion. My sculling technique wasn't much practised, but we made some headway using it as a sweep. The prospect of doing this for another 11 miles was a little daunting.

We drifted and rowed until a gentle land breeze picked up and we were able to work our way to windward, passing first Cabo Falso and then Los Cabos. We finally dropped the hook at 1:30 a.m. among the moored and anchored yachts which lay off the beach outside the holiday and fishing town of Cabo San Lucas. The water was deliciously clear, and we could see our anchor dug into the sand 25 feet below us.

Next to us in the anchorage were Tom and Thalia on *Sotto le Stelle*. Recognising their yacht's profile in the night, we had dropped the hook close by, and we were all pleased to catch up. Tom swam over in diving gear first thing to say hi, returning later with Thalia in their tender.

Later, Tom and Thalia showed us around town. They took us to the port captain's office, followed by the *aduana*, to finally clear immigration. After the isolated anchorages we had been exploring along the Baja coastline, Cabo felt like a city. With a population at the time of about 16,000 (which has risen today to more than 65,000), it was a favourite spot for tourists and the US sports-fishing crowd and had a reputation as a hectic party town. Located south of the Tropic of Cancer, it technically rated as a tropical destination. It was busy and dusty, and with all the construction in progress, it had a vibe of moving forward. The weather was noticeably warmer than even just a few miles north around the cape, where the northerly wind had a chill to it – we had entered a whole new weather zone.

We picked up a welcome pile of mail at Pappi's, a yacht-friendly cafe that operated as a quasi-base-station for the cruising fleet. Pappi's provided the cruising fleet with an address for a mail drop, and they had connections for spare parts and equipment to be sent from the States. They even maintained the daily cruisers' radio net for weather forecasts on VHF, also broadcasting any other relevant news. Pappi's had become the official meeting place and they did a roaring trade.

Here we met up with *Another Day* and *Callaloo*, with whom we had spent Christmas; also Jeff and Donna on *Keramos*, who we had bumped into a few times along the way.

A day or so after our arrival, an 80-foot ketch sailed in and anchored outside the line of smaller yachts. We were surprised to see the ketch's large inflatable tender make a beeline towards us, the occupants hailing us in a friendly manner. One of the guys introduced himself and the ketch's skipper, happily letting us know that he was an Aussie and had seen our ensign and come to say g'day (even bringing beer in the best Australian tradition – he was dismayed when I said I didn't drink).

Recovering quickly, Merv told us that he had lived in California for many years, and was crewing for his mate Dave, the skipper of the bigger boat. As we chatted – and it may have been at Merv's suggestion – Dave offered me a job on *La Madonna*, helping with maintenance and day sailing with guests while they were in Cabo. We were basically out of money, so the timing was perfect. I gratefully accepted the offer.

XVI

A Loss at Sea

ONE MORNING while I was working aboard *La Madonna* at Cabo San Lucas, the VHF radio was abuzz with chatter. The skipper of a yacht at sea reported on one of the ham radio nets that his wife had been lost overboard! He had been frantically searching the area alone, with no success, almost 200 miles south of Cabo San Lucas. The couple had been en route to Cabo from Isla Socorro when the husband came on deck at a change of watch to discover his wife missing.

By the time I heard this news, the skipper had been distraught and alone for more than 30 hours. He must have been insane with anxiety. I couldn't imagine what it must have been like for him. I had listened for a few minutes, becoming distressed not only for the owner of the 44-foot cutter but also by the casual-sounding nature of the conversation between boats.

Of course, everyone was concerned, holding their breath. Ham operators disseminated updates as the poor guy, Don, was relaying information to the US Coastguard and Mexican search and rescue authorities. Frustratingly, these SAR units were having trouble getting on station to assist.

The coastguard or navy helicopter, flying from San Diego, could only be on station for a matter of minutes before returning for fuel. The Mexican patrol boat also had a limited range, for some technical reason, so couldn't offer much assistance either.

Feeling quite anxious, I grabbed *La Madonna*'s radio mic, putting out a general call to the fleet. I offered that if one of the fast motor boats in the harbour had the range, some of us yachties could travel out with them to see what we could do to assist the distressed skipper. Perhaps we could help him search for his wife, or at least lend a hand with sailing the boat back to port.

Instantly, there were offers of help. A 48-foot powerboat owner replied, saying that they had enough fuel on board and were ready to leave immediately. Several other yachties offered to come along. I went back to *Deus Regit II* and filled Cindy in on what was going on (at that time our VHF didn't have the frequency to receive the local net) as I grabbed a few items, before being picked up by an inflatable and transferred across to the grey sports-fishing boat, looming large as it idled nearby.

In the tender was a guy who I liked instantly – he introduced himself as Doug Manheimer, from the sail boat *Halcyon*. There were about six men on board the sports fisher. As we powered out towards the search area we discussed possible scenarios, not knowing if we would be required to join the search or just assist Don to sail back to Cabo. At the least, we could put a team on board to support him.

All this happened very quickly. Radio operators on shore relayed to Don that we were heading his way, asking if we might offer some assistance and arranging a radio schedule for later that night when we were closer and within VHF range. We were heading for a position more than 150 miles out to sea. Later we were told that Don on *Golly Gee* had given up hope of rescue for his wife, Jan, and had reluctantly turned the boat towards the coast.

Soon after we left it grew dark. We powered along, averaging 18–20 knots – a far cry from our usual sedate progress under sail aboard *Deus Regit II*. It was like being in a pounding, bucking, wet tunnel, as the skipper had a huge spotlight aimed forward like a car's headlights. Driving down this tube of light, framed with spray and mist lifting from the bow wave, we were unable to see anything beyond the perimeter of the foredeck. We were navigating with what at the time was a brand-new device – a handheld Magellan GPS. A boat owner had come past in his dinghy, handing it up to me on the sports fisher as we prepared to leave, saying "This might come in handy." (They cost over $4000 at the time – not something you want to drop!) I'd never seen one before and none of us quite trusted it, so we plotted a DR on the way out to supplement the continuous update of the GPS!

After about six to seven hours, and closing on *Golly Gee*'s updated position, we slowed, scanning ahead with radar and keen eyes. All on board were silent as we peered into the black night. Finally we spotted a set of nav lights and managed to raise an exhausted Don on the VHF; he sounded relieved that we were there. Once on station, the owner of the sports fisher asked if it would be okay to send across two sailors, and Doug and I were transferred over in a small inflatable dinghy. It felt a bit like a navy SEAL raid as we clambered over the rail onto *Golly Gee*'s deck in the dark at 11 p.m.

Doug and I both felt like intruders. Don greeted us politely, as if we were regular visitors. His words were flat and spoken as if on autopilot; he was understandably confused and emotionally drained. He and the boat looked dishevelled. Don had been frenetically searching, sailing in circles with no rest or support for nearly two days. Uncoiled lines were strewn about the boat and partly furled sails hung limp.

Doug immediately put his arm about Don's shoulder supportively, and respectfully guided him below. He offered to make some hot tea and gently asked what Don wanted us to do. (A decision had been made earlier, in consultation with coast guard, that the search was to be called off.) Don seemed dazed, though resigned to leaving the area.

On deck, I went about sorting lines and tidying up the cockpit, preparing to get underway for Cabo. Meanwhile, Doug attended to Don, reassuring him that we would be okay with the boat and that he should get some rest. Once we were back on course the sports fisher escorted us for a time, picking up speed as daylight approached and planing off towards Cabo.

Arriving at Cabo San Lucas later that day, curious onlookers averted their gaze as we motored in to set anchor among the many boats moored in the crowded inner harbour. I had made a good friend in Doug that night, and we got to know Don as he processed his grief and began to take steps to deal with life after such a horrendous event.

We maintained contact with Don over the years. He hung about in Mexico for a few months, visiting us up in La Paz. He trusted us, I think, and would often share a meal. In 1996 he visited us in Newcastle on *Golly Gee* with his new wife, Lois, and had come to terms with his earlier misfortune.

XVII

To La Paz and
the Baja Bash

AFTER MORE THAN A MONTH in Cabo, we decided to head north to La Paz in the Sea of Cortez. It is a larger city with a more sheltered anchorage, and we hoped it would be a good, safe place to base ourselves and to leave the boat when I found yacht-delivery work. In company with *Halcyon* and *Orca*, we left Cabo, feeling flush having replenished the kitty by working on *La Madonna* caulking teak decks, varnishing, and doing general boat work for Dave. He was a ladies' man, a Robert Redford lookalike who lived the stereotypical sailor's cliché. One morning, on meeting his most recent flame, I asked him how he kept all the names straight. He replied, unfazed, "I call them all honey"!

La Paz lies about 150 miles north of Cabo San Lucas, into the Sea of Cortez or Golfo de California, on the inside shore of the Baja Peninsula. Once around the corner and about 50 miles in, we no longer felt the effects of the consistent Pacific swell we'd experienced on the way down from the States. Now these open roadstead anchorages had merit, providing better access for landing in the dinghy, without the threat of rolling over or swamping in the surf. The easier landing certainly made our stopovers more interesting and fun, as we could easily reach the beach for walks and to explore the fascinating arid desert beyond the dunes.

The one drawback was that now we were travelling hard on the wind, beating into the north to north-westerly that had been so helpful on the run south. We slogged away, tacking to and fro along the shore line. It wasn't long before our friends on larger boats, with reliable diesel engines for motor-sailing, had left us behind.

As we crept along the beach just a few hundred metres offshore, trying to stay out of the chop, I was puzzled when our progress came almost to a halt. Was this a current eddy or were we trying too hard, pinching up too far to windward and causing the sluggish progress? The mystery was solved when I noticed a large fish hooked on the line trailing astern. The drag from the fish, combined with the already choppy motion, was enough to stop us altogether as we pitched and punched into a nasty short chop.

I had almost reeled in the fish when the line broke! The culprit got away and *Deus Regit II*, released of her burden, started to gain ground. But after a while we copied our friends and fired up the outboard to give us an edge in our battle against the current, wind, and chop, to rejoin our friends at our first overnight anchorage en route to La Paz, at Los Frailes. Even though we had only left them a few hours before, it was fun to catch up and discuss the day.

We broke the remainder of the trip to La Paz into three legs, leaving at around midnight to take advantage of the calmer conditions and hopefully make better time; even so, it was hard going once the wind got up. The next leg took 18 hours to cover just 50 nautical miles, tacking in the short, sharp seas to arrive at Ensenada de los Muertos (Bay of the Dead). Our friends gave us a victor's welcome in the evening, as we had let *Halcyon* know that we had landed a dorado (often called mahi-mahi or dolphin fish) as long as the cockpit floor. We had plenty to share. An impromptu pot-luck dinner was arranged, with the largest boat in the bay being designated host, and we all enjoyed a barbeque on *Baba Barann* – a new boat to us – whose American owners welcomed our small group as we dinghied over to share the meal.

Yachts anchored in La Paz – a beautiful sunset

La Paz was a nice place to settle for a bit. It was a large city, and the capital of Baja California Sur. Although it was bustling and busy, with around 130,000 people, it didn't feel like a big city (although of course there was no comparison to the small, quiet villages we had visited on the way). Many buildings were humble, with a mix of paved and dusty streets, and the people lived simply. We were there for work and planned to stay longer than our other stopovers, giving us time to get to know people in the town as well as the transient yachting community.

Various people we had met on our trip down the coast sailed in and out at various times. We were always running into friends from other boats, enjoying updates and meeting new crews, often discovering that we had mutual friends.

We were anchored in front of the landmark Hotel Los Arcos, a short walk along the attractive *malecon* (esplanade) to the markets and town centre. We met Mike and Karen Riley for the first time. This couple had just completed a circumnavigation of the world aboard their 24-footer, *Tola*, a simple little boat that made *Deus Regit II* look sumptuously appointed. They had a 19-month-old son, Falcon, and he and Annie became good mates. Martin on *Orca* called in for a couple of weeks, before heading off to the Marquesas in French Polynesia, en route to Australia.

We fell into a routine, getting to know the city, becoming regulars at our favourite cheap restaurants and places to shop at the markets. We found a good clinic where we could maintain Annie's regular checks and vaccinations. Annie was a favourite with everyone we met; her blonde hair and blue eyes always drew attention as we went about town. She learnt to play on this, and would throw off her hat and watch expectantly as passers-by would pick it up and chase after her.

If you had a child in Mexico, it seemed you were immediately accepted. We were always greeted warmly, and Cindy was especially made to feel respected, whether it was an official's office, a restaurant, street vendor, or market stall. At the markets, Cindy had become friendly with a number of the female stallholders; they would send her off to do her shopping while they looked after *la niña*, letting Annie play on the floor with their own children or grandchildren.

One of our priorities in La Paz was to find yacht delivery work. It was a bit early in the season when we arrived, but it wasn't too long before I got a call via the office of Marina de La Paz to be in Cabo San Lucas the following day to help sail a yacht to Newport Beach in California.

The first time I made the 'Baja bash' – the return trip back to California against wind and seas – was to provide a real insight for me. I felt slightly spoilt as I spotted my ride: *Ole* was a Santa Cruz 70, a sled-class ultra-light racing yacht, and I was to join the crew of three others for the trip back up the coast. Bill Matchett was the skipper; also on board were another Aussie, Rossco McDonald, and a young deckhand. I got on well with them all, and the almost 800 miles beat to windward were remarkably uneventful. But I was impressed with the power and authority of the much larger, faster boat, compared to our small floating home.

One night we were forced to shelter behind a headland in gale-force winds, heading out again the following morning after we'd all had some rest. The conditions outside had not changed much, but we were able to make progress and keep to schedule. We sailed when we could, with a blade jib and the reefed mainsail, or, when the wind headed us, using the sails in combination with the engine for a boost through the hard, lumpy waves.

We covered distances in an afternoon that would have taken two days in similar weather on *Deus Regit II*. While steering as we rounded Cabo Falso, I was impressed when the boat launched off the top of a wave, feeling the stress loads distribute through the boat's structure as she crashed back down with hardly any loss of momentum. I thought then that these light, modern boats were indestructible and wonderful!

For such a big boat, the size of the gear was manageable, and it sure was exciting to sail. With some thoughtful adjustments to layout, even a boat like this could be set up for shorthanded or solo crews. Food for thought: a 50-footer could only be better, and what I learnt went into my BOC bank of concepts and musings. I was forming a sure conviction that I wanted to work towards the BOC Challenge. Even so, we were a long way from home, and with a young family and no money it did seem a little unrealistic.

About this time, I had an experience that added fuel to the fire. We had met an older American businessman sailing quite a radical cruising boat – a one-off Farr design based on a sharpie style. It was a prototype, long and lean, and it sailed very fast. The owner had been hoping to tap into the developing market for a new type of performance cruising yacht.

At some point, it came up that I was interested in doing the BOC race, and he offered us the use of his boat, suggesting we could modify it to suit the maximum length requirements. He felt he had the contacts to get sponsors to cover the cost of the modifications to the boat and wages for me, and he would lend us the boat as a promotion. This all seemed too good to be true!

Cindy and I had talked between ourselves but hadn't spoken much to anyone else about my aspirations for the BOC, yet here we were in the boondocks, and we had stumbled across a possible benefactor. If everything went as discussed, we thought we could just pull it together in time for the forthcoming race in September that year (1990).

He asked me to meet him in San Diego when I was back up that way on a scheduled delivery. But when I contacted him to follow up, it was apparent that his enthusiasm had run its course. I heard talk of financial problems and dodgy deals and our patron had become elusive. The meeting never took place.

I learnt from that experience; it was another part of the process that helped me garner the information and the will to build a plan to pursue the goal regardless.

After the trip on *Ole*, I was busy that season making repeated yacht deliveries back up to the States for owners who didn't have the time or the inclination to tackle the return journey after enjoying a winter in Mexico. One owner had to be medevacked back to the States, and I helped his wife make the beat back to San Diego to truck the boat overland to their home in Oklahoma.

On another occasion I had taken on a 36-footer that needed to get to California, and started the passage with the girls, making a stop in Cabo. Once we were out of the benign Sea of Cortez and into the rough stuff outside the peninsula, the boat started to fall apart. The autopilot failed, hatches leaked, and, more seriously, a torrent of water started to flood through the heads, where the corroded seacock couldn't be shut off.

When the boat was heeling over, hard-pressed in a big gust, it was the last straw. Six-month-old Annie, wedged snugly into the settee with cushions around her, suddenly tumbled off, bouncing across the cabin to end up under the table. Cindy scurried around to retrieve her as I instantly put the helm up and gybed around to head back to Cabo. I was giving up on the 100-odd miles we'd worked hard for, but I was suddenly full of insight as to why the owners didn't want to make the trip themselves.

I took the girls home to La Paz on a bus, then hired another sailor who had been keen to get some more experience. I also found a couple of young boys from Michigan who had been backpacking around Mexico for a post-graduation adventure. We dealt with some of the boat issues while waiting for the winds to ease, then took off early one morning, making good time in much better conditions than we had when Cindy and Annie were on board.

Later in the season, Cindy and Annie again tried making the bash with me on the lovely 32-foot yacht *Velero*, which Cindy and I had admired soon after we arrived in La Paz. The boat was being taken north to be sold. We had previously met the owner, who asked us to make the trip for him. We took this as a chance for our families in Australia to meet Annie. As Cindy's younger brother was also about to be married, we decided to fly back home after the delivery to California and introduce our daughter to her extended family.

The passage on *Velero*, while not having the same potential for disaster as the earlier trip, was interesting to say the least. It was hurricane season, and we had to watch for tropical storms forming behind us. Fortunately no big winds materialised, but a large swell was running, evidence of some serious weather further south.

The dense tropical weather behind us seemed to suck the air out of the region, replacing the usual fresh northerlies with light winds. This made the trip easy, though it meant we were reliant on the engine to get us north as soon as possible.

We also had on board an English backpacker named Colin, who was along for the adventure and to assist with watch-keeping. All went well from La Paz to Cabo, but less than 30 hours into the leg north from Cabo San Lucas, on the open Pacific side, we discovered that two of the mounting brackets for the engine had broken. The motor was sitting aligned in place reasonably well, but if we had been under sail and heeled there was a real risk of the motor jumping out of alignment and becoming unusable.

We carried on, with a tight set of cord lashings on each of the engine mounts holding the motor down and others tied diagonally in each direction to resist any torque, or twist, from the motor. With no choice, we made a stop at Bahia Magdalena, travelling a further 20 miles up the channel to Puerto San Carlos, a small town and shipping port for coastal trade. We hoped there might be some mechanical services, or the possibility of flying parts down from the States. We made the trip in a fog-like drizzle up the winding, narrow channel, where the nav lights conflicted with each other and our charts. We anchored late at night, just off an old merchant ship tied to the wharf.

Ashore, in the morning, I met the engineer from the Greek (Panamanian flag) freighter *Galini* that we had noticed as we arrived, telling him of our plight.

He offered to come and look at the mounts, arriving with tools, unbolting the defective brackets, and taking them back to his ship. The engineer welded a metal strap to join up the cracked top and side plates – a repair that we hoped would hold up for the remainder of the trip. We were thankful that we could get sorted so quickly.

The captain of the ship invited us to dinner with the crew. Interestingly, several officers had their wives and families visiting on board from Europe, so it was more civilised than the rough exterior suggested.

Back on track, the benign conditions persisted and we were able to keep to our schedule. However, only 260 miles later, just before arriving in Bahia San Bartolome (Turtle Bay) – the mental halfway point for the bash – I noticed that the engine mounts had failed again. We made it in okay and had them re-welded by a tradesman in Turtle Bay village. When the engine mounts were re-bolted in place I doubled things up with additional lashings, just in case.

Passing to the east side of Isla Cedros, still without wind and motoring along in thick fog, we were jolted to attention as a speeding fishing panga came tearing up out of the mist alongside *Velero*. The lone occupant was gesturing wildly for us to stop. The fisherman had no idea of his position, and he said that he was on his last drops of gas. Could we help him out? We weren't much better off than him as far as position fixing was concerned, running our dead reckoning through the fog, but his situation could have become quite serious. He was less than half way along his 15-mile course from a camp on Isla Navidad to Isla Cedros. When we met up he had already been set off course, and had he continued he would have been floating around somewhere in the bight between Cedros and the coast 50 miles to the east, in an area known for strong currents.

Annie inspects the LORAN aboard Velero, *off the Baja coast heading north*

We took the panga in tow, and Diablo (apparently his nickname) jumped on board for lunch. When asked why he had left for the trip with so little gas he shrugged, indicating that they did it all the time. We altered course, and after an hour and half some buildings came into view out of the mist at the salt loading facility on the southern end of Cedros. Our new friend jumped in his panga and took off inshore to get some fuel to finish his trip. As a thank you, he left us four abalone and hastily mimed instructions on how to tenderise and prepare them for cooking.

The weather was cooperative and we made good time with no more problems, though the engine mounts were a constant worry. Little did we know that our biggest adventure was about to begin.

Arriving in San Diego to clear customs into the country, we were met with the immigration officer from hell. When he and his colleague arrived at the boat, moored alongside at the police dock at Shelter Island, I was concerned when he put his hand on his holstered gun and told me to "Stand back!"

They boarded the boat and asked for our paperwork, which was in order, and then declared that we were illegally in America and that I was in breach of laws in regards to the operations of US-flagged vessels. I had already cleared into San Diego several times that season at the same dock, but this time the officer advised us that we were to be detained on board and could not go ashore, at the risk of a $4000 fine – per person!

I argued (very politely) that Annie was in need of some nappies and that we were out of food after the voyage, among other things. (There was a great diner nearby, and we had all been thinking of hamburgers and milkshakes for a few days.) I told him that San Diego was an intermediate port and that we still had about 180 miles to sail to our destination. The officers left and would not complete our entry process.

We had no instructions apart from that we were to stay on the boat. Poor Colin had planned to leave the boat in San Diego and continue his trip, but he was stuck with us. After several days of 'confinement' on the police dock (largely ignored – we did go shopping and also to the diner, where the hamburgers were as good as expected), each day making phone calls and trying to get some advice, we received word that we could continue to our final destination – though still with our entry formalities incomplete. This was all well and good, except that we were headed up the coast past Los Angeles to Channel Islands Harbour, and there were no customs or immigration services in that port. When I pointed this out, however, we were told to leave regardless.

Speaking with Larry, the owner of *Velero*, and his broker, we decided to keep going and hope we could work it out in a few days' time. Once at Oxnard, we were put in touch with a senior officer from Border Patrol who interviewed us and raised the issue with his counterpart in San Diego Immigration. On review, the immigration officer we dealt with admitted to having "over-reacted" in our case. Nothing could be done to reverse the decision or our current status, as the order for our detention had to be "finalised in the system". We were to be escorted out of the US in the yacht owner's custody.

It all sounded very serious – but in fact, with the consent of our border patrol contact, we simply jumped on a bus and left via the nearest border crossing, only to re-enter a short while later through another gate.

I must have had face for slap as, once again, one of the officers was hostile and demanded to know what we were up to! She had noticed us exiting not long before, and decided we were up to no good. We started to explain the situation – that we were under instruction and were merely completing a formality. Eventually she was prepared to allow Annie to enter – being a Canadian citizen by birth – but Cindy, Colin, and I remained anathema and could not pass go.

Fortunately a more friendly and reasonable person intervened, who seemed to have a little more clout. She gently asserted some authority over the other agent and calmed things down. Our helpful agent number two asked us to explain again and she must have decided we measured up, as she moved the first agent to another booth and said we could enter, but maybe keep a low profile next time we were doing a quick in-and-out in that tense border crossing.

Finally back in the 'land of the free', we parted company with Colin. I am sure he enjoyed getting back on the road and mixing with other backpackers who might not lead him astray as much as we had. We continued overland to San Francisco to visit Steve and Marja, before picking up our flights back to Australia, where we had a fantastic reunion with family and friends who we hadn't seen for almost three years.

XVIII

Atlantic Voyage and
BOC Challenge HQ

RETURNING TO LA PAZ nearly three months after we had left aboard *Velero*, we found *Deus Regit II* about half a mile from where we had last seen her, on a different mooring to the one we had rented before leaving! No one had any idea how she came to be there, and the small gouge along her topsides didn't offer any clue either.

En route home to *Deus Regit II*, while we were still in California, we had called in to see Dave 'I-call-them-all-honey' Kettenhofen, the skipper of *La Madonna*, at his place at Newport Beach. He'd bought a 55-foot yacht on the East Coast and was heading to the Caribbean to charter her. Dave was excited about the new project and asked if I would be interested in helping him take the boat to the British Virgin Islands, and if I would fly over to Boston with him the following week.

It was very short notice! But there was enough time to settle Cindy and Annie in La Paz before I left again. Back on board *Deus Regit II* in Mexico, we rented a berth at Marina de La Paz so that it would be more convenient for Cindy to live alone with the baby.

I travelled back to San Diego and flew to Boston with Dave, and from there we drove 'up state' to Gloucester, Massachusetts to pick up the boat – a nice, modern 55-foot cutter called *Quintessence*. We sailed to Marblehead and Provincetown, then via Cape Cod Canal to Newport, Rhode Island. I was particularly interested in visiting Newport as the 1990–91 BOC Challenge had started there a few weeks earlier, and I was hoping to call in at the race office to see how the event progressed and learn as much as I could.

I was happy that we were gale-bound in Newport, giving me free time to hike out to the race headquarters at Fort Adams. I had phoned ahead and spoken with Pete Dunning, the race's communications director, and he had invited me to visit.

Pete was highly regarded in yacht-racing circles and had been involved with most of the early single-handed transatlantic races and each of the previous editions of the BOC Challenge. Showing up at his office, I was a little hesitant as I was aware that he must have spoken with a heap of 'dreamers' over the years.

I told Pete how I planned to sail in the next edition of the race in 1994, and felt encouraged that he appeared to take me seriously. He proudly showed me the communications system and demonstrated how the race office was able to keep a close eye on the competitors, with updated positions of each of the yachts by ARGOS transponder and through regular radio schedules where the skippers logged in each day.

The timing of my visit was uncanny: while I was in the room with Pete, an emergency radio call came in from the Australian entry in the Open 60, *Interox Crusader*. The skipper, John Biddlecombe, was having rudder troubles off the coast of Brazil near Recife, and he had decided to abandon racing and divert to Bermuda for repairs, effectively ending any chance of continuing in the race. I couldn't understand it – the distance to sail to Bermuda was almost the same as remained in the leg to Cape Town. That incident affected me profoundly. Hearing the with-

Pete Dunning, the race coordinator, at BOC Race Headquarters. Pete was always happy to discuss the event and his – for the time – high-tech nerve centre.

drawal as it unfolded over the radio made me acutely aware of how difficult the race might be, both in terms of competition, and the personal challenges involved.

Once back at sea aboard *Quintessence*, I felt a real empathy with the BOC fleet as they raced down the South Atlantic with us following their progress. Each day we tuned the SSB radio to the AT&T marine operators as the BOC yachts logged on, filing position reports to the powerful shore station 'Whiskey Oscar Mike' (WOM). I listened, rapt, and was convinced deep in my gut that in four years' time I would sail in the next edition of the race.

The voyage with Dave, his new wife Barb, and the good old Aussie, Merv, whom we had first met in Mexico, went well. We stopped to catch our breath for a few days at the incredibly beautiful island of Bermuda, waiting for some serious weather to pass; then we sailed direct to Tortola in the British Virgin Islands. It was a nice voyage overall, though we did have some strong winds, and it increased my big boat experience. I loved being on watch alone on deck as we sailed under spin-naker at 11–14 knots of boat speed. I felt that all these events and seemingly chance encounters were part of a bigger story shaping my future prospects.

XIX

New Directions

BACK ON BOARD *DEUS REGIT II* in La Paz, Cindy and I discussed the things I had learnt in Newport and on that voyage. I had to confess to her that I had arrived home empty-handed: being naive I hadn't made any financial arrangements with Dave prior to signing on, and at the end of the trip he simply thanked me, handed me air tickets, and sent me on my way.

Merv, noting this exchange, was embarrassed and sheepishly slipped me some cash, saying "Here's some travelling money, Al." Although I appreciated this, it was far short of what I had expected to earn for my time and efforts on that job; and in addition, a large chunk of my work opportunity for the season was gone. However, it was a momentary setback and we didn't take it personally. Instead, we focused our attention on considering what our options might be if we were to commit to the BOC Challenge in four years' time. Like most plans, this one started out small and grew, creating its own momentum.

Initially, we talked about building a boat to suit the minimum length allowed – 40 feet. Don McIntyre, one of the Australian entrants in the 1990 BOC Challenge, was sailing the Adams 50 *Buttercup*, and he marketed a fibreglass version of the similar, though smaller, Adams 13 design. We thought that the 43-footer might be a perfect fast long-distance cruising boat, as well as being suitable for the race. I had brought back some brochures and magazine reviews from our visit to Australia, and would often re-read these while pondering the possibilities.

We hatched a basic plan that felt achievable: first, sail back to Australia instead of going to the Caribbean, as had been our intention. If we sold *Deus Regit II* and I could earn decent money working in the bush again, or on a construction project, we could probably scrape together enough to buy a fibreglass Adams 13 hull and deck and fit out the boat simply ourselves, with minimal furniture and no engine or cruising equipment. This would save money and keep it light.

Once the boat was under construction, we felt sure that we could put forward a suitable case to find sufficient sponsorship to complete her in time for the 1994 BOC Challenge.

It was November 1990, and we had more than 8000 nautical miles to sail before we could actively advance that goal. However, we took a step forward by committing to stage one – which was to set sail back across the Pacific for Australia the following March, when the southern hemisphere cyclone season had ended.

Meanwhile, we continued to enjoy life in La Paz, cruising to some of the local islands and other nearby destinations when we had time between jobs.

Annie had been able to scramble her way around the boat for several months now, with plenty of easy handholds within reach. Now she was walking and enjoying the extra range. She also loved the sandy beaches. One day at Isla Partida, north of La Paz, she was playing in ankle-deep water while we looked on when Cindy, looking down from a high rocky ledge, suddenly cried out for me to pick her up. I grabbed Annie just as a small sea snake slid along the sand in the crystal water, centimetres from her feet! From a safe distance up the beach we were happy to watch the deadly sea snake move off, showing little interest in us. A bite from it would certainly have proved fatal.

Commuting in the new Montgomery dinghy we accquired in La Paz – this tiny tender was the perfect fit for our boat and growing family.

While we started talking among our friends about our decision to return to Australia the coming season, we didn't initially share our new, bold plan and my intention of entering the round-the-world race. At that stage, it seemed too far away and a little out of context to our current position. I did share the idea with Susan Hiscock and Christian Bastke and both voiced the same sentiment, Susan by letter and Christian during a phone conversation: "Why do something so stupid when you are already enjoying a fantastic adventure with your family!" I couldn't really argue with that.

So we kept it to ourselves. There was a lot to do before the goal could become a reality, and we knew we had to take one step at a time.

From La Paz we sailed south again to Cabo San Lucas, where we had arranged to meet some friends from Canada on the boat *Seeadler*. We retraced our steps to Bahía de Los Muertos (Bay of the Dead) and Los Frailes, tearing south in strong northerlies and some of the most vicious short, steep waves I have ever come across, and so close together that we corkscrewed down the face of each wave only to plunge into the back of the next one.

In Los Muertos we met up with Steve and Marja Vance aboard *Twiga*. The Vances were en route to the Caribbean via the mainland coast of Mexico and Panama, and we hoped to spend Christmas with them somewhere on the mainland side of the Sea of Cortez.

Our Canadian friends Ulrich and Margo on *Seeadler* had taken longer to reach Cabo than expected. We had arranged to meet in early December as they were carrying some items for me that I had bought recently in San Diego after a delivery trip. Like us, they cruised off the grid without long-distance radio and so were unable to update their ETA. We were unsure whether to wait, or to leave and try to catch up with *Twiga*.

Eventually *Seeadler* arrived, and it was worth the wait to see Margo and Ulrich again. We had become friends in the Gulf Islands in British Columbia. Ulrich was Swiss, and an exceptional engineer and boat builder. Margo was an artist, so their boat, a traditional double-ended ketch, was unique and immaculate. While we waited in Cabo, we enjoyed the beaches and caught up with old friends we had met the season before, as well as meeting many new people who were arriving.

One boat that I recognised, though I had only spoken with them by radio as we passed each other north of Isla Cedros on a delivery, was *Destiny*. I noticed that the 44-footer had arrived in Cabo and, rowing past, I greeted Dana, the owner, introducing myself with reference to our VHF conversation when I was on *Circe* the previous season. Dana's wife, hearing my Aussie accent from down below, barked my name sharply.

She came on deck muttering about revenge! She recalled that I had given them a bum steer that day off Cedros, months before. On my 'recommendation' they had left the anchorage and bashed away all day in conditions they didn't enjoy. I had merely said, in perhaps an understated way, "It's not too bad out here", as we beat north in the little yawl I was delivering, in 25-knot head winds and lumpy seas.

I guess sometimes it is better not to give an opinion. We had been making headway, and trying to maintain a schedule, so didn't want to stop and delay. When the much bigger *Destiny* motor-sailed past us several hours later, and I saw their bow rising and crashing down off each wave, I realised how rough it actually was. Paula had apparently vowed at the time that when she saw "that Aussie" next he would be in deep trouble. We all had a laugh, and enjoyed regularly crossing paths along the mainland coast over the following months.

My BOC aspirations were further encouraged in Cabo, when we met the very experienced sailors Mike and Pat Pocock from the UK. They were sailing *Blackjack*, one of Mike's own designs. He was very interested in the BOC race and the evolving style of fast boats for solo events. He told us of a new, radical 35-footer that he had drawn for English solo sailor Mary Falk, and he described how the boat *Q II* was water ballasted and capable of 200-mile days, with the aim of winning its class in the famous OSTAR race. He was familiar with the Adams designs, and showed us drawings for one of his 45-footers that was similar in detail to the Adams 13 we liked so much. We enjoyed meeting this enthusiastic couple and I appreciated Mike's insight into yacht design and performance sailing. It seemed like I was gently being coaxed along, meeting people in an almost small-world scenario and picking up insights and information that was both interesting and added to the thread encouraging my BOC aspirations.

XX

Mainland Mexico

BEFORE HEADING BACK OUT into the Pacific, we planned to sail 800 nautical miles further south and east as far as Acapulco. We sailed via a small island, Isla Isabela, where we saw migrating Californian Grey Whales breaching and where we spent 24 hours at anchor, surrounded by thousands of raucous sea birds. Crossing the Sea of Cortez from the Baja Peninsula to what was referred to as the mainland, or the Pacific coast of Mexico – about 280 miles – we moored about a mile inland, up a well-marked channel, off the small town of Puerto San Blas. It was a lovely river inlet and safe harbour located north of Puerto Vallarta. We moored among a dozen or so yachts, seven of which we had met before. It was Christmas Eve.

Back in Cabo, we had noticed that Cindy seemed to tire easily, and as we wandered around San Blas on Christmas morning with the crew of the yacht *Mere Image*, she was feeling unwell and light-headed. Visiting a restaurant bathroom, she discovered she was spotting heavily. With everything shut for the day, we frantically tried to find a doctor. Back on *Deus Regit II*, Cindy decided some bed rest would be helpful.

Under Cindy's instructions, I cooked Christmas lunch, which turned out surprisingly well. Compared to the desert terrain and climate of Baja, the mainland coast was tropical – lush green and densely humid. We weren't used to it, but we enjoyed the change.

Finding a doctor a day or two later, I remember sitting in a dark timber-panelled room of a colonial-style building on a steamy, humid day, with the doctor reassuring us that Cindy was okay and giving us the surprising and delightful news that she was more than likely pregnant and should take it easy.

Still digesting this wonderful news, we continued our journey, drifting pleasantly along in light winds, making short hops so that Cindy could rest, and using anchorages marked on the charts behind headlands or in a curve of beach a bit deeper than the trend of the coastline. We often needed to use two anchors, one out forward and the other from the stern, to hold our bow aligned into the swell that wrapped around the adjacent headland, thus minimising rolling. We anchored in the lee of Punta Chacala, then La Cruz (La Crux de Huancaxtle), and for a taste of urban life we sailed over to the popular town of Puerto Vallarta.

At each of the major towns – or anywhere there was a port captain's office – we had to clear in and out with officials, almost as if we were arriving in the country for the first time. This always involved multiple copies of documents, and repeated visits. Though a complex process, it was also a bit casual; often we were able to check in and out on the same day, even though we weren't necessarily leaving for some time. The sequence varied with each port: first *inmigración*, then to the *capitanía del puerto*, to *aduana*, back to the *capitanía del puerto* again – or any variation of the above. The offices were usually located miles apart, and the process typically involved several hours. Even so, the officials were always friendly and interested in what we were doing. They didn't seem to notice how redundant and laborious the bureaucratic process was. All we could do was comply.

In Puerto Vallarta we caught up again with Rick and Marilyn, whom we had first met on *Tortuga* in Alameda. We were disappointed to learn from them that our friends on *Twiga* were by now a couple of hundred miles ahead of us and ready to leave for Costa Rica en route to Panama and the US east coast. After several days in Puerto Vallarta, we sailed 15 miles back to La Cruz for some peace and quiet away from the city. There we celebrated our second New Year's Eve in Mexico. It was 1991.

Moving south across the Bahia de Banderas, we were happy to sail past the notorious Cabo Corrientes – another local 'Cape Horn' which has a reputation as being difficult to get around – with nice winds and calm seas.

As we sailed along the deserted beaches, a series of huge, palatial homes overlooking the water south of Careytos dominated the landscape. The architecture ranged from Moorish to modern, looking out of place on the barren coastline. We were intrigued by these few imposing, almost fortified-looking mansions spread over many miles of coast and evoking thoughts of feudal barons and castles in old Europe. This turned out to be the local 'millionaires' row'.

Further on, in Bahia Navidad, we ran into Doug and Nancy Manheimer on *Halcyon* again. We hadn't seen them for several months, since La Paz. They had further explored the Sea of Cortez before making their way down the mainland coast, while we had stayed in La Paz making yacht deliveries north to California. They were both keen scuba divers and infectiously enthusiastic about everything, and we enjoyed their company. Now we were headed in the same direction; we each maintained our own pace, leaving when we were ready and seeing one another along the way with no pressure – if this was buddy boating, it was okay with me. We said farewell to them further along the coast as they left Bahia Navidad on a nonstop hop of 200 miles to Zihuatanejo, where we looked forward to catching up with them.

Later, as we sailed out of Bahia Navidad, a couple of miles offshore we came across a fisherman rowing an old wooden panga about 12 feet long. Coming alongside, we offered him our old 2-horsepower dinghy outboard, or *motor fueraborda*. It had been randomly uncooperative for a while and we had been thinking of dumping it, as we hadn't had any fuel for it (due to budget restrictions) for some time. Knowing how resourceful people can be when not reliant on workshop manuals and service agents, we thought that he would probably make better use of it than us.

I handed the motor down from our boat to the small, rough panga as it momentarily banged up against us, and the delighted fisherman quickly clamped it onto his boat's transom and proceeded to pull the starter with a determination that was inspiring. I had told him clearly that it wasn't working properly, but that I reckoned he could sort that out. Smiling, he said something about his brother being a *mecánico* and he waved us on.

Las Hadas was a huge 2000-room resort, with a couple of hundred condos and complete with its own yacht harbour. It was located a few miles across the bay from the busy commercial port of Manzanillo, and we had planned to break our trip there. Cindy was still quite run down, so we were trying to keep the sailing legs as short as possible.

We were surprised to see *Halcyon* anchored off Las Hadas as we made our approach and sailed the anchor in, after enjoying a fantastic five-hour sail with warm, easy winds that held all the way into the anchorage. Doug and Nancy had changed their minds, deciding to stop off as well. We didn't argue with that, and enjoyed sharing a meal with them on board *Deus Regit II* that night. Las Hadas had a St Tropez feel to it – expensive and indulgent – as we walked along the boardwalk docks among several large yachts and motor boats moored Mediterranean style, with anchors forward and stern lines to the shore.

Even though we were at anchor, and not bona fide hotel guests, we were allowed to use the resort facilities. The girls enjoyed relaxing with fresh hotel towels on sun beds by the huge landscaped pool. It seemed a little unreal, and highlighted our financial position; we had been down to our last – literally our last three 1000-peso coins – for several days. I was not sure when we would have the opportunity to earn some money again. We hoped that something might present itself in Z-town, or maybe Acapulco, as groups of yachts seemed to congregate there.

Enjoying an overnight sail of 120 miles, where we carried the spinnaker for the entire trip in flat seas and a steady breeze, we anchored in the bay off a small village in Caleta de Campos (Bufadero Bluff), late one afternoon. Although we did have staples – rice, flour, sugar, and tea – we felt stressed to be low on fresh provisions, which we hadn't been able to buy for some time.

For some reason the idea of no bananas (Annie's favourite) was having an impact on the household that day, and I went ashore with Annie to give Cindy a break. I was determined to come back with something to contribute, taking a couple of T-shirts and some other items with me, with the vague hope of swapping them for some fruit if I found a store. Up the hill, overlooking the anchorage, was a small village and an even smaller *tienda*. I put our pesos on the shop counter and asked what I could get for that, offering the T-shirts in a gesture indicating that I was interested to trade these as well.

The lady in the stall caught on pretty fast: she took what I had in my hand and proceeded to load the counter with fresh produce! It wasn't my proudest moment, but I felt like the proverbial 'hunter home from the hill' as I rowed back with Annie and eight bananas, a dozen eggs, seven tomatoes, and a kilo of potatoes.

As I raised the anchor at midnight and we started to silently drift out of the anchorage at Bufadero Bluff, heading for Zihuatanejo (Z-town), the large, dark, ominous shape of a stingray glided underneath *Deus Regit II*; it was beautiful in the clear water and moonlight.

But Zihuatanejo was a long time coming. We had expected to arrive there the following afternoon, but the wind was light and we barely drifted along the shoreline; becalmed for several hours, we were even being set backwards by the current. What little breeze there was flicked around, occasionally from ahead, and then from behind. All the next day and through the following night we ghosted along.

In the morning, 30 hours after leaving, we spotted *Halcyon* coming up on us from astern. They had left Las Hadas a full day after us; while we had stopped for eight hours to rest and 'reprovision' at Bufadero Bluff, *Halcyon* had been able to motor sail at a steady pace. We entered the wide bay that is Zihuatanejo, having taken 32 hours to sail and drift 80 miles, which I think was a record for us.

XXI

Zihuatanejo (Z-town)

TIMING IS EVERYTHING. As we sailed into the bay, even before we had picked out a spot to anchor off the *playa* Zihuatanejo, we tuned into the 8 a.m. cruisers' net on the VHF radio (by now we had upgraded and had a radio with the correct international frequencies). I couldn't believe my ears when a yacht called *Horizons* expressed a wish to buy some charts of the Caribbean. I immediately called back via the net and let *Horizons* know we had some charts available. We anchored next to *Halcyon*, and near to our friends Donna and Jeff on *Keramos* and Rod on *Pegasus*. I had last seen Rod leaving Neah Bay in Washington, 17 months before.

Within an hour Andy, the skipper of *Horizons*, had collected 24 charts of the Caribbean that we no longer needed as we had decided on the westward route back to Australia. Nobody had any idea how critical that transaction was to our economy; Cindy and I were thankful to have money again (US$80) to keep us going a little longer. Even better, Rod put me in touch with a yacht that needed some repairs, and I spent a day and a half scarfing in and fairing a teak section of the damaged cap rail of *Sabrina*.

In another example of providential timing, Mark, the owner of *Sabrina*, introduced me to his boss, who owned a charter yacht operating in the bay. Mark was keen to leave for Costa Rica and wanted to hand over a replacement skipper before he left, to soften the blow. Within a week of arriving in Z-town, I was the skipper of the charter yacht *Las Brisas del Mar*, copping some flak from Tousley on *Keramos*, who suggested that I may have sold out, running a tourist boat.

The holiday-makers were all having fun and I was thankful to have what amounted to a regular job for the first time in nearly two years. I didn't have to leave the girls to fend for themselves for weeks at a time, and I arrived home with cash in hand (on advice from my predecessor) at the end of each day. After the recent lean period our cruising fund was now growing at a great rate.

Each day we sailed to Isla Grande, about 7 miles up the coast. The guests

Skippering Las Brisas del Mar – *a timley job that helped fill the cruising kitty for our return passage across the Pacific*

would lunch ashore at a local restaurant set up in a *palapa* (a thatched roof, open structure) on the beach. Lunch was followed by a swim and then a relaxing sail home. In the evenings, we loaded *Las Brisas del Mar* up for a sunset charter. Weaving our way around the bay, we would pass the anchored cruising yachts, including our friends who were dismayed to find themselves on display while relaxing and enjoying their evening in the cockpit. They would have to smile nicely while the charter guests gawked, dreaming of what it might be like to live on board a yacht and sail to exotic locations.

Our mail had been sent to Acapulco, care of the Club de Yates, as we had expected to be there sooner. But we were hesitant to leave the bounty of Zihuatanejo, needing to keep working as long as possible before jumping off on the next leg to French Polynesia. Luckily, friends of *Halcyon* on the yacht *Perihelion* had kindly picked up our mail in Acapulco. As always, we were happy to hear from our families and friends. I was particularly pleased to receive a letter postmarked Lanester, France. It was from the solo sailor Jean Luc Van den Heede, who had sailed in the 1986–87 BOC Challenge, standing out as a formidable competitor skippering the very narrow (8′4″) 45-footer *Let's Go*.

I had written to Jean Luc, asking some general questions about the race and about his boat, whose design I admired; she was light, narrow, and very fast. *Let's Go* had come second in Class II, beating several of the bigger and more powerful first division Open 60s. I was thrilled to receive his friendly advice and good wishes. It was another link in the chain that kept me connected, motivated, and confident that I could make the BOC Challenge a reality.

Zihuatanejo was a traditional Mexican village, in contrast to the resort town of Ixtapa only a couple of kilometres over the hill, with its huge skyscraper hotels built on the beach. Most of our charter guests flew into Ixtapa from the winter regions of the United States and Canada, relieved to see some sun and feel the warm tropical water. They landed in this manufactured ambiance, with its whirl of hotel night clubs and restaurants, and seemed limited to enjoying activities on the beach and around the pool. They missed out on the authenticity of nearby Zihuatanejo and meeting the real Mexican people, who we were fortunate to get to know and enjoy.

We had become friends with the crew working on *Las Brisas del Mar*, Jose Manuel and Adriana, who were taking time out from their 'real' jobs in the film industry in Mexico City. We enjoyed attending their wedding ceremony on the boat. This was followed by the festivities of a traditional reception, including the bride dancing across the tables, at Porto Mio, the restaurant and private dock where the charter boat was based.

We had also been befriended by a couple who owned two local Italian restaurants and who had a toddler about Annie's age. They invited us to dine at their main restaurant in Ixtapa one evening. It was a bit fancier than our usual street food or *palapas* on the beach, so we dressed in our best. It took three attempts to land in the dinghy (the surf was up), and I had to return to *Deus Regit II* twice for dry clothes, both of us changing on the sandy beach. Fortunately we had left Annie in the care of some friends anchored next to us. We were pretty ragged and less than relaxed by the time we arrived, by taxi, at the restaurant. But putting these logistics behind us, Giuseppe's didn't disappoint, and we enjoyed a nice meal on the house and had a pleasant evening.

Around the middle of March, Doug and Nancy on *Halcyon* said their goodbyes, departing for Hiva Oa, one of the French Marquesas Islands. *Keramos* was leaving soon for Costa Rica, and other friends were scattering in various directions. It was time for us to move on too.

We had a loose challenge with *Halcyon* that the boat with the slowest time for the passage to the Marquesas would cook dinner when we caught up next. But first we had to sail to Acapulco, where I had planned to haul *Deus Regit II* for new bottom paint and general maintenance before embarking again on the broad span of the Pacific.

After almost eight weeks of steady work and of enjoying the relaxed pace of life in Zihuatanejo, I put in my notice with the charter company and, with little to do to prepare for departure, we were ready to go.

Cindy had spent a couple of big days canning, using a technique she had learnt for preserving produce and meat. We were stocked up for the voyage ahead with 22 Mason jars of preserved meats such as chicken and pork, tomatoes, carrots, and other vegetables that would remain fresh, healthy, and nutritious out on the open sea. No more scurvy-like symptoms for us, we hoped!

Cindy and Annie were happy to be underway again. Z-town to Acapulco was only a 110-mile passage, which we covered in 19 hours of wonderful sailing – one of those rare days when the sea is flat without a ripple, but there is enough wind to sail effortlessly at maximum speed. Arriving ahead of schedule, we hove to for a couple of hours, awaiting daylight to enter the harbour. In the calm morning, we passed outside Isla Roqueta, making our way around to the Club de Yates de Acapulco, where we were booked to use the slipway to haul out *Deus Regit II* for fresh bottom paint and a maintenance check.

Acapulco was busy and congested. The dramatic, steep hillsides were crowded with houses and hectic narrow streets. Emerging from the quiet of the yacht club precinct was always an adventure. It was a real contrast to the barren and remote Baja, or even the simple west coast ports we had visited and loved.

The haul-out and boat work was straightforward, and soon we were back in the water preparing for the passage to French Polynesia. We took time out to explore the city – just a taste really – by bus and foot, walking one evening to La Quebrada, a popular tourist attraction where young men climb without ropes up the 100-foot-high cliffs, before diving into only 11 feet of water. Gauging the timing of the waves rolling into the little inlet is crucial before taking the plunge.

It was now the end of March, and with the cyclone season in the South Pacific officially over, we set about leaving. Cindy being pregnant caused a little concern among the people we knew, though her attitude was always so upbeat, and our lifestyle so natural to us, that neither of us had given any thought to her not sailing the passage, at least as far as Tahiti.

We did delay our departure for two days as Annie suddenly developed a stomach bug, which was unusual for her. Her tummy was as tough as nails from chewing raw onions and chilli, given to her when teething by the Mexican women in the La Paz markets who looked after her when Cindy was shopping. Cindy put her on a 'BRAT' diet of bananas, rice, apples, and toast, and she responded overnight. We waited a day for her to settle – and this day was also Cindy's twenty-fifth birthday.

All seemed well with Annie as we weighed anchor and set out on the almost 3000-mile voyage to Hiva Oa in the Marquesas.

XXII

The Pacific Westward

USUALLY, BOATS LEAVING the west coast of Mexico make their departure from further north and west, often up near Puerto Vallarta or even Cabo San Lucas. But we knew of other boats that had left from Acapulco, and they had had a reasonable trip to the Marquesas. We anticipated lighter winds for the early stage of the passage, but had no idea how light they would be. Considering the options, it didn't make sense to sail back the way we had come, and we felt that any slower progress would be made up by not backtracking.

A few miles out of the harbour, I was dumbfounded to see that the Sumlog (knot meter) had stopped working again. We had fitted a new cable in Canada, after sailing most of the way over from Australia without a way to measure our boat speed or log the distance travelled. Here we were, embarking again on a major voyage, and once more the cable had broken. At the time, the old-style mechanical Sumlog was being made redundant by electronic speedos overtaking the market, so it had been difficult to source the cable and we had no spare.

It had been luxury to have the Sumlog working for the mostly coastal sailing we had been doing from British Columbia, even though we could track our position using regular landmarks. And it did contribute to the accuracy of the dead reckoning and celestial navigation. But now we would have to go back to estimating our speeds, making the dead reckoning a bit arbitrary, with no log record to balance our guess of distance per hour or day's run. I was a little frustrated, to say the least. It certainly wasn't a disaster, but I had hoped to be as accurate as possible.

Even so, by this stage we were good at estimating the speed of *Deus Regit II*, and we would often check by measuring the time it took to pass a floating object such as a ball of paper thrown off the bow, but it did mean our accuracy would suffer over the coming four to five months of sailing.

Leaving late in the afternoon, we took it easy, settling everyone in for the passage, and enjoyed reasonable sailing. The sea was lumpier than we expected, even with the light wind forward of the beam, and the following day our noon position put us 86 miles along our way. Later, we spoke by VHF to a US warship that was hovering nearby, and they gave us a position report which fit neatly with our sun sights.

All through the first night and the following few days, the wind was tapering off as we cleared the influence of land, and it continued to be fluky and light. We were able to hold our course, but progress dropped off accordingly. After four days we had only made tentative steps forward, with less-than-startling daily runs – on that day we made only 28 miles towards the mark, which really pulled the average down!

Light, fickle breezes were to become the order of the day; it seemed we were in the stranglehold of a feeble breeze that only allowed us to creep across the chart. Navigation consumed a big chunk of the day and often showed little result for the hours spent on deck trimming sails, tacking, or gybing as the wind flicked about.

To add to our worries, Annie's stomach bug had returned with a vengeance; she had diarrhoea again and was back on the BRAT diet. We considered turning back, but by then the wind and swell had swung around to come from the north-east and it would have been an uncomfortable, difficult, and slow beat back to Mexico. So we procrastinated, expecting that it was a temporary malady and that Annie should soon pull through. She would recover quickly after her food intake was limited, and we would be encouraged – only for the symptoms to suddenly reappear a day or two later. It looked like our supply of nappies wouldn't make the distance.

It was disheartening to see Annie unable to hold down any nourishment, though she was otherwise in her usual good spirits. Apart from the diarrhoea, we could identify no fever or other symptoms. We kept up her fluid intake and consulted a medical book that we had on board. The book concurred with our treatment regime of restricting food and the BRAT diet, so we carried on.

The light winds persisted, and we jogged along at a pace much less than our target averages. Ocean sailing tends to make you an optimist. If you were out there second guessing yourself and looking at the negatives, it would get old quickly. Weather is dynamic and usually won't stay the same for very long; but this time we seemed to be trapped in a stationary system that was frustratingly not the norm.

Patience and optimism become part of the process – waiting for the winds to pick up, or expecting that the seas will calm down. Knowing that a change is inevitable makes it possible to keep looking towards the next day and the next position or milestone along the way. Marking off progress provides a sense of achievement and satisfaction when voyaging.

We had previously made arrangements to listen in on our radio receiver to the ham Maritime Mobile Net, to track *Halcyon* and several other boats we knew which were also sailing towards the South Pacific, either ahead of or behind us.

One evening we heard Doug on *Halcyon* check in and report their position. They were about 19 days into their crossing; we were a couple of weeks behind them by the time we had sailed to Acapulco, worked on the boat, and were ready to make our departure, and were now a few days into our passage.

Even though we could not speak to them, it was always exciting to hear of our friends' and others' progress, and we enjoyed the one-sided camaraderie. One evening we heard two boats that we knew, having met them on our route along the Mexican coast: the first boat, *Kodiak*, was a fast performance-orientated 35-footer; the second boat, several hundred miles astern of them, was a 42-foot, more traditional, heavy-displacement vessel that had suffered a broken boom.

I was impressed when *Kodiak*, realising that the boom problem was causing their friends more stress than it perhaps required, offered to standby. In fact, they turned and sailed a converging course to offer moral support and suggestions as their friends dealt with the unexpected setback. *Kodiak* kept up a reduced pace for the rest of the voyage to the Marquesas, remaining available to provide comfort and/or assistance should their friends need it.

This action was certainly above and beyond, as the damage to the boom only affected speed and handling but didn't really endanger the vessel or the safety of the friendly older couple on board. This kindness on *Kodiak*'s part reinforced the relevance of the traditional law of the sea, that one mariner will offer help to another in times of trouble. *Kodiak*'s willingness to act was just one example of the sense of community that develops among cruising crews as they move about the planet in sync with the seasons.

The downside of listening to the radio as we drifted along was that we heard boats south of us on the other side of the equator coming from Galapagos or Panama towards the Marquesas. They were tearing along in fresh south-east trade winds, making impressive daily runs that emphasised the lack of progress in our equatorial ramblings. But it did give us hope for a better future, reminding us that eventually we would reach those same steady winds.

We celebrated my twenty-eighth birthday after another uncomfortable night rolling and rattling about in an unusually choppy sea with tantalising, but barely useable, easterly winds. Annie's tummy bug struck again; nevertheless, Cindy made the day special, preparing a birthday feast topped off with a freshly baked carrot cake and some fun presents for me and Annie.

At the end of week three, we had barely reached the halfway point of a voyage that we had anticipated might be sailed in only 28 days! The light winds and adverse currents held us in their grip, showing little remorse. We tried to glean information on what conditions to expect by listening to other boats checking in from various locations, as well as from weather reports on WWVH, in an effort to track the position of the fickle Intertropical Convergence Zone – the area of doldrums – and determine the best place to cross the equator. But with so little speed to position ourselves, it was a patience game we had little control over. Sometimes a gale is easier to deal with than calms. At least you have plenty to do in the build-up, and can adopt various strategies that give an illusion of 'control'. During one of these glassy days I decided to have a swim. I dived in, and Cindy passed 18-month-old Annie down to me, attached to a safety line. We admired *Deus Regit II* drifting by.

It was actually a little unsettling to be floating in the almost three-mile-deep water; the feeling was akin to a fear of heights. I felt quite removed from the safe shell of our little floating home. Annie was usually fearless in the water, but she must have picked up on my discomfort as she displayed an awareness of our unnatural position too, and let us know in no uncertain terms that she preferred to be put back on board immediately. Even so, it was refreshing dip.

The following day I went aloft to inspect the masthead and rig. From 30 feet above, I saw a shark swimming lazily below our hull, before disappearing into

A mid-ocean swim – not as restful as it looks! There is something surreal about miles-deep water.

the depths. Maybe Annie knew something that I didn't as we floated in the swell beside the boat the day before.

In addition to Annie being unwell, Cindy had been losing weight for some time and was about 23 weeks into her pregnancy when she began to lose blood and experience painful contractions. We were both very worried. We had a boat that wouldn't budge, and two people with potentially serious health issues on board.

We consulted the medical book (*Advanced First Aid Afloat*, P. Eastman) again to get some insight as to what may be happening. There was a section on childbirth and miscarriages that offered a gloomy, though practical, scenario that I had trouble processing. I felt out of my depth.

The book described specific medications to be given intramuscularly; we had neither the medication nor the skill to administer it. Challenges are often faith-building exercises, and we felt a little stretched trusting that Cindy and the baby would both be okay. We took solace in the fact that Cindy was not bleeding as profusely as Eastman's book indicated, and I made her as comfortable as possible, there being nothing else we could really do.

In fact, the light winds were a mixed blessing. With the gentler motion, the boat was stable and Cindy could rest in the forward bunk. When she had had complications with Annie at about the same stage of her pregnancy, Cindy had been to hospital for several days and was subsequently confined to bed rest for several weeks. Even though this time the symptoms were different, we adopted the same strategy and hoped for the best. Meanwhile, we tried to keep some food in Annie's system as her irregular vomiting and diarrhoea continued. We prayed for some breeze to help put this passage behind us.

This was probably the only time that we regretted not having radio communications on board; it surely would have been helpful to get some advice. But in all reality there wasn't much that could have been done so far out to sea. We took inspiration from the words of a famous Bob Dylan song we like, and kept 'pressing on'. On day 22 we celebrated our fourth wedding anniversary and the skies were clear for the first time in over a week.

There were still the ordinary things to deal with – navigating and sailing the boat, as well as keeping an eye on maintenance. One day I spent two hours stripping the motor because it wouldn't start; I cleared cooling waterways, changed spark plugs and cleaned the carburettor, to no avail. Days later, in frustration, I gave the starter an angry pull and it turned over and ran first time!

Not that we could motor anywhere, but it was important to keep the systems in working order. The engine chugged away for an hour in the glassy calm, making five knots and barely putting a dimple in our distance to go.

The mainsail had been giving me trouble for a while. The slugs that attached the luff of the sail to the mast had worn and were binding in the track as it went up or down. In an effort to have them run better, in the calms I removed the sail and re-seized all the luff sliders so that they couldn't move out of alignment. Generally, though, the boat was reliable and the least of our worries.

I was confounded by the persistence of the light winds; we trickled along, making 50–80 miles a day. Our fixes plotted on the small-scale chart seemed to mock us, and certainly didn't offer much encouragement, marking our daily runs off, it seemed, by the millimetre. For a time, south-westerly headwinds created a lumpy, uncomfortable, confused sea. One day we would pick up an eddy of favourable current, only to be held back the next day by the unhelpful North Equatorial Countercurrent.

We caught rainwater as we passed under thunderheads, hoping for some breeze in the squalls. Some days we meandered along with barely steerageway; in one six-hour period making only 5 miles. I was thankful that we had painted the bottom before leaving, and knew we had done as much as we could to ease *Deus Regit II*'s way through the water.

While we were stressed, it wasn't all dire on board. Towards sunset most evenings the girls would congregate on deck, sitting forward on the upturned dinghy and enjoying the world passing, albeit slowly, by. A pod of spinner dolphins regularly showed up over several days, entertaining us by leaping high out of the water and spinning their bodies furiously, before splashing down to start the process again. They seemed to like our attention and I guess, being more than 1500 miles from the nearest land, they were happy to have an audience. Frigate birds followed us regularly, dive-bombing the boat and attempting to land on the aft end of the bimini and perch there like piratical parrots, only to be disturbed as the flapping awning canvas lifted and shooed them away.

Progressing slowly towards the equator, we would pick up a furtive breeze, hinting at a breakthrough, with a noticeably longer day's run; then the breeze would vanish again. It was hard going, squalls and light patches outweighing any advantage from the occasional scrap of useful breeze. As we closed on the equator, determining by our noon sights on day 25 that we were only 42 miles inside the Northern Hemisphere, the breeze finally showed signs of cooperating and we had our best run of the passage so far, sailing 130 miles over 24 hours.

This was fabulous; our little boat could do these averages – she just needed a consistent breeze. It was a huge contrast to the conditions we'd been experiencing, and encouraged us to think that soon we would be over the line and making better time. We calculated that we would cross the equator in the evening, and this was cause for celebration. It seemed we had been focused forever on the elusive equator; now, crossing over, we were relieved to be suddenly enjoying better conditions.

We marked the occasion with an equator party. Cindy produced a package that Doug and Nancy had left with her to mark the moment. The parcel contained some games and balloons for Annie, and a hand-painted banner that read "You're back in the south!" which we blu-tacked up on the cabin overhead liner, creating a festive air.

The following day we were a little disappointed to have only made good another 88 miles, but that was short-lived, as the winds settled and blew steadily from the east-south-east. Picking up momentum, it felt like the starting gun had gone off and we were now in a race. We never looked back for the remainder of the leg, with each day's run exceeding the previous one.

Two days after crossing the line, we were elated to mark off that day's run of 153 miles; the end was in sight, and we were confident that the trade winds were finally established and would see us in soon. Even with the great progress, we both

Back in the South! Ecuator party en route to the Marquesas

felt burdened by concern for Annie and for our new baby struggling to develop. It was urgent that we find safe harbour and medical assistance.

On the evening of day 32, with sights of Venus and Jupiter, we calculated that we had only 95 miles to run. In the morning we picked up the steep, barren, rocky, almost 365-metre-high sentinel of the uninhabited Ilot Fatu Huku, which was our arrival point. We altered course to pass around the eastern end of the island of Hiva Oa and proceeded to the anchorage at Baie Atuona: we had arrived finally in the Marquesas!

Our passage had taken 33 full days, and it was with some relief that we set the hook under sail. More than 30 boats were anchored in the bay when we arrived, most from the Europa Round World Rally. Among the other boats we spotted *Destiny*, with Dana and Paula on board.

The leg had been a challenge for us all – the slow sailing conditions themselves were not really a problem, but combined with Cindy's and Annie's health issues, it had been a frustrating time. It had taken almost 25 days to sail the first 1800 miles, but we had covered the remaining 1200 miles in less than nine days, which spoke well for our little ship when she was in the groove.

XXIII

French Polynesia

THE MARQUESAS are a group of high, mountainous, lush green islands, with dramatic, steeply sloped volcanic peaks. They are located on the eastern edge of the French Polynesian Territories, straddling the line of 10 degrees south latitude. First settled by Polynesians over a thousand years ago, they are arguably among the most beautiful places on the planet and have had a strong attraction for sailors since the first European ships stumbled across them in the late sixteenth century. It was a huge relief to arrive.

We went ashore to visit the *gendarmerie* at the village of Atuona and check into the country, receiving three-month visas and directions to the hospital.

Here we met a woman doctor from France who had been in the islands for a couple of years. She was concerned about Cindy's weight loss, contractions, and the bleeding she had experienced over the past few weeks, and suggested that Cindy should take it easy. She felt she could help us stay in the islands to have the baby, with excellent facilities available if we wanted.

She also had a solution for Annie's troubles, diagnosing her with giardiasis (a parasite that takes up residence in your intestines), and prescribing two tablets – one to be taken immediately, and a second dose 20 days later. We saw immediate results: the diarrhoea abated and Annie's skinny little body quickly began to regain its healthy roundness. Cindy was still very run down and, with no pill to cure her, we decided it would be best if the girls flew back to Australia, where Cindy could check in with a doctor and focus on getting well.

Getting the girls home became our priority. It was hard to get a flight out of the remote island group as locals had priority and the aircraft always operated at maximum capacity. It was rare for a seat to become available at short notice. However, our good doctor contacted the airline, confirming that Cindy had grounds for priority evacuation on medical reasons. The airline was helpful too, making room on an upcoming flight for Cindy and Annie to fly the 1200-odd kilometres to Tahiti, where she could connect with direct flights to Australia.

During the little over two weeks that we were together in Atuona we got to know Olivier and Marie, a Tahitian couple who were based there with Olivier's job as a meteorologist. We got talking with them one day while walking to the village and, with typical islander generosity, they invited us to their home, where Annie played happily with their children. Before we left they loaded us up with fruit from their garden, sending us home to *Deus Regit II* with arms full of delicious *pamplemousses* and lemons.

At the post office we received mail from home addressed to *Deus Regit II*, Yacht in Transit, Poste Restante Atuona. As always, it was special to get news of our families after weeks of no communication. We heard on the grapevine that *Halcyon* was exploring some of the islands to the north before heading for the Tuamotus, and also that *Seeadler* was visiting Fatu Hiva, only about 40 miles away – but too far for us to head over in our current state. For several days we were in and out of the village, faxing back and forth to Australia and moving money about to arrange tickets and schedules for the girls to make connections from Papeete to Sydney.

It was bittersweet to see Cindy and Annie off at the airport. It would be hard to be apart again; however, it would take the pressure off us both, and it would cer-

Anchor down in Atuona, Hiva Oa, Marquesas – the bay looking empty after about 20 Europa Rally yachts had left!

tainly provide peace of mind knowing that Cindy could get medical attention and rest to regain her health and strength at her parents' home in Newcastle in time for our new arrival. For me it was also a relief from the constant worry and guilt I felt for bringing on the hardships of our seafaring lifestyle.

After seeing the girls off from the airstrip cut high into the ridge atop the mountainous island, I set about getting the boat and myself ready to leave and started looking forward to the passage home. Our cruising was coming to an end, but sailing nearly 5000 miles single-handed was a good ending and would be excellent preparation for the BOC Challenge and a challenging experience for me. I saw it as a way to assure people that I was capable of taking on the solo race.

That night I was invited, with many of the other visiting yachties, to a barbeque at the house of one of the local chiefs. I was feeling a bit out of it without Cindy along, so was just hanging out on the periphery of the crowded room, observing the good mood of the other guests, when I noticed a news report come on the flickering satellite television (unexpected and seemingly out of place) in a corner of the room.

I was drawn to the vision on the screen of a racing yacht that I recognised and, realising it was a French news broadcast, was amazed to see that it was about Isabelle Autissier's recent arrival into Newport, Rhode Island, as she completed the 1990–91 BOC Challenge. Isabelle had finished in seventh place after being set back by a dismasting earlier in the race, though she had managed to make repairs and stay in the competition. It was thrilling, being in such a remote location but watching a news report about the race I was planning to enter. The timing felt auspicious, on the eve of my single-handed voyage to Australia.

XXIV

Solo to Papeete

CINDY WAS DUE to have the baby at the end of July, and it was mid-May as I prepared to get underway. I had a window of less than ten weeks to sail almost 5000 nautical miles. I planned to stop in Tahiti, the Cook Islands, and maybe Tonga, so that I could keep in touch by making the occasional phone call to Cindy and even collect or send mail if the timing worked out.

Weighing anchor and departing Atuona felt quite different to my earlier experience on the US West Coast, when I sailed single-handed down from Canada. I didn't have the pre-voyage jitters that I experienced then; the next 800-mile leg to Tahiti was a continuation of the current voyage, so the transition was less intense.

The boat was noticeably quiet without the girls on board, but I felt confident and excited to be underway and was looking forward to seeing how I would go under the pressure of our new, non-negotiable deadline – to get myself and *Deus Regit II* home in time for the birth of the new baby. I slipped into 'delivery mode', focusing on the job at hand. In effect, our cruising days were over for the time being and a new chapter of our life was unfolding, though I didn't give it any thought at the time.

I opted to sail to the north of the Tuamotus before altering course to pass down the western perimeter of the region once known as the 'Dangerous Archipelago'. This name was given on account of the difficult navigation among the reef-strewn low-lying coral atolls. These narrow, circular coral reefs enclose often large lagoons dotted with *motus* – small islands – where the highest point may be a coconut tree. They are hard to see from the deck of a small boat until you're almost on top of them. The region's fearsome reputation was exacerbated by its unpredictable currents.

With the advent of satnav and GPS this is no longer such an issue, but at the time, as I was relying only on celestial navigation, I intended to skirt the edge, keeping well clear of the area. The passage was free of obstacles and quite straightforward. After feeling a little isolated on the first day, I soon settled into the solo routine of watch-keeping, navigating, and resting when I could.

It's a key priority to conserve your strength at sea, especially when sailing alone. Even with Cindy on board, when we first left Australia I had a tendency to burn out about ten days into a voyage. I would sometimes crash, my body craving a respite from the constant state of alert; of perpetually keeping watch and paying attention to sail trim. These times of accumulated fatigue were at first a surprise, and would creep up on me. Cindy learnt to see this coming and would occasionally extend her watch, allowing me to sleep for a couple of extra hours uninterrupted to refresh myself.

We quickly learnt to pace ourselves – especially me, as Cindy was always good at shifting gears to get some rest. We managed our energy levels by taking regular breaks and resting when appropriate. Even on those magical days when the crew, the boat, and the sea were in harmony and you felt like you could sail forever, adequate rest was as much a priority as safe navigation and regular maintenance.

The key to this, really, was to ensure that we always had sufficient reserves to sail safely under deteriorating weather conditions or during a difficult navigation phase – such as when making a landfall or passing an obstruction. By now it had become natural for me to read my body clock and pace myself, so that fatigue was rarely a problem.

On the fifth night of the leg to Tahiti I was sailing in light winds, with only enough movement through the water to maintain steerage way. I had opted to sail between Mataiva, the westernmost Tuamotuan atoll, and its neighbour, Tikehau. The shortcut would save me several miles, and the channel between the two atolls was about 22 miles wide, offering plenty of room for a safe route to cut the corner. Importantly, keeping more to windward of my course would allow me to sail freer for the last 150 miles to Tahiti, where I would be hard-pressed into the trade winds and compensating for plenty of current set as I headed, close-hauled on port tack, towards my destination.

My navigation calculations so far on this leg had been coming in well and had been confirmed by various methods and celestial bodies with agreeable accuracy. However, I was sailing in an area known for erratic currents. Drifting along around midnight in a flat sea, with a beautiful bright moon to light the way, I had been comfortably asleep, pleased with my good progress and knowing that in a few hours I would be able to turn the corner and make for Tahiti. I was awoken when the bow was suddenly lifted by a subtle swell coming from a direction inconsistent with the conditions at the time. Immediately alert, I was on deck in seconds. I could feel a regular wave motion that was barely discernible looking at the flat sea. It was coming from the direction of the reef surrounding Tikehau, which, according to my evening star sights, should have been at least 12 nautical miles on my port side. From the section of jagged-edged horizon visible in the moonlight, it was clear that the fringing reef of the atoll was much closer than my course allowed for. Evidently there were stronger currents in the area than I had anticipated, and the boat was being sucked towards the reef.

I could see the white backs of waves crashing onto the reef; the reflected return of the wave motion was what I had felt nudging the boat as I slept. Altering course more to the west, to compensate for the current that had forced me to the left of my track, allowed *Deus Regit II* to drift clear as we continued on our way. The flat sea made for ideal conditions as I shot and reduced moon sights to firm up a line of position. I was thankful for the tap on the shoulder that had made me sensitive to the unusual wave pattern and helped us avoid becoming a statistic attesting to the reputation of the 'Dangerous Archipelago'.

Nearing Tahiti, the south-east trades increased in strength and *Deus Regit II* had a bone in her teeth, making good time heeled over in the steady breeze.

Tahiti is a mountainous island. Its peaks, rising to over 2000 metres, could be seen from a great distance, announced by the gathered clouds surrounding the island. As I sailed towards this high cloud and my destination of Papeete harbour, I came under the influence of the wind shadow created by the island, sailing late in the afternoon across a visible line with breeze on one side, and absolutely no wind and smooth water on the other side.

Inching closer to the pass into Papeete, I started dreaming of calm anchorages, a full night's sleep, and delicious, cheap Chinese food from the small mobile catering vans, called '*le truck*', that lined the waterfront. Just after sunset, I could smell food from *les trucks* wafting across the water, and I actually sailed *Deus Regit II*'s nose up between the channel markers, lining up the leading lights on the shore that defined the entrance of Passe de Papeete. So close and yet so far! The boat was sucked back out by the outgoing current, visibly burbling past the floating buoys.

The outboard motor was out of action with cooling problems, leaving me no choice but to turn about and drift a safe distance offshore before heaving to. I spent the night with the sails backed, off the famed Point Venus, waiting till morning for a second attempt at entering the pass.

In the early light, I was dismayed to again face the same predicament – no wind, and an adverse tidal stream barring my way into the harbour. Contemplating my options, I was delighted to see a black-hulled, Canadian-flagged yacht motoring up to the pass in the calm. I was more pragmatic than proud as the couple on board threw me a line, towing me towards the main town quay, where I could see *Halcyon* at anchor. Doug and Nancy gave me a warm welcome as I cast off the tow and drifted up to drop anchor next to them in time for breakfast.

Papeete has always been a favourite destination of mine, and I was happy to arrive safely and check in at the port captain's office. I was greeted by a guy about my own age who had been on duty the first time I had arrived, in 1980, aboard *Spindrift*; and again when I had sailed in with Cindy nearly four years previously. He seemed to recognise me too, and we smiled our mutual recognition.

I was used to the system there, which made things easier and speeded up the check-in process. Rifling through the held-mail box, I picked up a letter Cindy had left me before she and Annie had joined their flight to Sydney the week before. She sounded upbeat, writing of her adventures staying in a hostel with only curtains for room dividers, and describing some of the characters who had slept on the floor next to her and Annie's foam mats. A dodgy experience perhaps, but certainly cheap. Considering Tahiti is one of the most expensive countries to visit, Cindy had been surprised to find affordable accommodation while waiting for the flight.

I was able to speak with Cindy by phone and hear that she and Annie were settled at her parents' place, and that she was in the care of a doctor and on course to be fit in time for the new baby's arrival.

Knowing that the family was safe and settled, I had a day or two off and took care of some jobs on board – mainly sorting the cooling problem with the motor. Being a purist is one thing, but being forced unnecessarily to spend an extra night at sea wasn't such good seamanship. I spent some money on a new water pump impeller and repairs to the electronic ignition, hoping to have a reliable motor for the rest of the passage home.

Doug and Nancy and I enjoyed catching up for the first time since Mexico. As the slowest boat to the Marquesas, *Deus Regit II* owed *Halcyon* dinner, but I think, given the absence of Cindy and her great cooking, they didn't hold me to our bet. I ate with them each night, either on board or at *les trucks*, and no one had to suffer my cooking!

XXV

The Cook Islands

I PLANNED TO SAIL the remainder of my journey westward to Australia in three legs, with breaks in the Cook Islands and Tonga, before tackling the Tasman Sea for the winter approach to Australia.

Doug and Nancy waved me farewell, and I headed out in the early afternoon to clear the Passe de Papeete, initially opting to sail to the south of Moorea. Tahiti's smaller sister, Moorea is located about 15 miles downwind.

The channel between Tahiti and Moorea is usually quite lumpy, as the South Pacific swells and currents are compressed between the islands. True to form, the channel contained uncomfortable rolly seas, exacerbated by the lack of wind as I again drifted within the wind shadow of the larger island. My plan was to motor for a while until I was out of the windless zone, but I felt frustrated when the motor overheated and cut out – so soon after the recent repairs!

Deus Regit II was defenceless in the rolling swell and strong current; I was rapidly being set towards Moorea and her fringing reef. Even though I had plenty of sea room for the moment I was nervous, aware that if the wind didn't fill in soon it might be impossible for me to steer clear of the reefs.

When I spoke with Doug on the VHF radio, he offered to come out and give me a tow. It would have been an ignoble start to the passage, but I was giving serious thought to accepting his kind offer, as the situation felt pretty dire. After an anxious period of trying to coax *Deus Regit II* on course in the zephyrs and contrary sea state, I was hugely relieved to notice that a plastic bag was wrapped around the engine leg and propeller, blocking the cooling water ports – hence the overheating problem.

Once relieved of the offending plastic bag the engine started and ran as it should, and I was able to motor-sail clear of Moorea. By now it was close enough that I thought it prudent to sail to the north of the island, keeping the reefs to windward, rather than risk the possibility of being set down again by the strong current. Eventually free of Tahiti's wind shadow, and with the sails drawing, I felt that we were really on our way, with spray on the bow and the tell-tale vibrations that kicked in when *Deus Regit II* sailed fast.

The leg to Rarotonga in the Cook Islands was only 620 nautical miles on a mostly south-westerly heading. I was expecting the south-east trades to be a nice beam reach and that we would make good time. Not to be taken for granted, the trade winds became uncooperative and, after a good first night sailing clear of Moorea, they dropped away, tending to blow more easterly. Once again, we were just trickling along in soft airs.

Listening to a Radio Australia broadcast, I was pleased to hear an interview with David Adams, an Australian who had recently competed in the 1990–91 BOC Challenge aboard the 60-foot *Innkeeper*, placing sixth overall. I was fascinated to once again hear, in so remote a location, a news article on the race I was planning to enter. I listened, rapt, as David described his adventures and talked of his intention of racing again in the 1994–95 BOC – due to begin in less than three and a half years. There is nothing like a deadline for motivation; I felt a sense of urgency, aware that my race to get to the BOC start line had already begun.

It is great to have plans and contemplate new adventures, but I needed to focus on more immediate issues. Not long after David's motivational sound-bite, we were becalmed again. The winds had gone around to the westerly sector for a while and had become fluky. It took all my effort to keep *Deus Regit II* moving; we trundled along, averaging only 1 knot of boat speed for the following 24-hour period.

When the trade winds came back they did so with a vengeance, and we sailed hard for the remainder of the passage in boisterous, reinforced trades of over 30 knots. While the comfort level on board was diminished by external conditions, at least we were back up to speed, ticking off real miles with a heavily reefed mainsail and small jib set.

Six days after leaving Tahiti, the tops of Rarotonga cleared the horizon and I was thankful for another perfect landfall. A few hours later the craggy volcanic peaks of 'Raro' were clear enough of the horizon to identify, and I was able to confirm my position by vertical sextant angle and then firm up the course to close with the coast with only 22 miles left to run.

Being unable to make it to the harbour at Avarua – the main town on the island – before dark, I hove to for the night in relative comfort, enjoying the sight of lights ashore in town and sheltered from the fresh trades by the lee of the land.

Rarotonga is the southernmost and largest of the Cook Islands. Its name actually means 'down south', which is how the early Polynesian navigators referred to it.

Avatiu Harbour is a small, artificial basin, the entrance having been cut through the fringing reef. Large enough for small merchant ships – mainly from New Zealand – to berth alongside, there were two other yachts tied to the rough concrete wharf when I sailed in, early the following morning. It was a neat little harbour, with some small fishing boats and enough room for one or two more boats to anchor closer to the shore. The only issue was that it was totally open to winds from the north and north-west. I couldn't see that this would pose any problems, considering the steady south-easterly tradewind region in which we were situated.

I would remember making that observation again a few nights later, as the wind shifted and blew straight into the harbour, accompanied by a big rolling surf. Poor *Deus Regit II* was beaten up against the dock wall – by the time the wind had hit us it was too strong and choppy to move the boat. In desperation I managed to heave my spare kedge anchor out from the side and, with it set, hold us off the wall by about half a metre. In spite of this, *Deus Regit II*'s topsides suffered several significant dings and scratches. It was fortunate that the waves were rolling in perpendicular to the sea wall: we were pitching up and down violently as the swells rolled under us, with an occasional bang against the wall. If the angle had been different

Bashing up on the sea wall in Avitua Harbour, Cook Islands, as an untimely nor'wester blew hard one night, causing some havoc for the yachts caught out tied alongside.

it would have been a disaster, with the boat lying against the unforgiving concrete dock.

The big steel Italian 45-footer *Lea*, moored a few metres ahead of me, made an awesome sight as one minute its transom would be higher than my topsides, then it would drop below, swapping places as the boats surged up and down in the ferocious seas. It was a bonding experience shared with Eduardo and Brunella on the other boat, as we all were on deck fending off. Needless to say, no one got any sleep that night.

Clearing in and out of customs was easy in the Cooks, but there was one odd rule visitors had to abide by: a local driver's license was mandatory (whether one planned to drive or not), so I had to buy one. Putting it down as an expensive souvenir, I also used it as a good excuse to rent a small motorbike and tour the island. I don't really make a good tourist, especially travelling alone, but it was fun to get out and explore with a bit more range than my legs could normally do in a day. I enjoyed the view out over the lagoon as I rode the small CC scooter around the circular perimeter road, then ducked up random trails leading inland through the dense tropical vegetation to higher ground to see what I could see. Typically, the locals gave friendly waves or indicated that I should stop and chat, curious as to what had brought me to the Cook Islands.

After five days pinned in due to the rough weather, I was ready to move on, always aware of Cindy's impending due date. I enjoyed our phone calls from these stopovers immensely; it was so good to hear her confident voice and know that her health was improving.

XXVI

Towards Tonga:
The Friendly Isles

THE LEG FROM RARO TO TONGA was plagued with contrary winds and heavy southerly swells. Covering about 900 miles in ten days, there was little evidence to suggest we were even in the tradewind belt. A large low-pressure trough persisted in the area, and the prevailing helpful winds were replaced with westerly headwinds, causing me to tack to and fro across the course line and thus increasing the distance I had to sail.

I was excited as I made my exit from the small basin at Avarua, sent off by Eduardo and the crew on board *Lea*. I was starting to feel like I was nearing home, with only one more stop to make on the itinerary. (The reality was that I still had further to sail than I had come since the Marquesas.) The forecast was for moderate southerly winds, and as I turned onto my course the winds were from the west at about 8 knots. It took some time to clear the reefs that embraced the island. I was hoping that the wind would shift to the more favourable southerlies soon, as I pushed into a six-foot swell and chop from the south-west. I must have been in a good mood, as I wrote in my journal that it was a beautiful day. My opinion changed as I started to bang away upwind.

Even though we had only been gone a few hours it was important to establish an accurate start point to begin the navigation for the leg, to confirm that the instruments were working and that the dead-reckoning plots were falling into line. I did this before nightfall; it placed me about 13 miles on my way.

That first night out, I heard friends on *Achates*, last seen in Zihuatanejo, check in on one of the single sideband radio nets I had started to monitor as I moved closer to Australia. Single sideband frequencies (SSB) are similar to ham radio and are used for ship-to-shore and ship-to-ship transmission, being long-range, high-frequency units. They operate on specific frequencies available to anyone with an operator's certificate and these are a bit easier to get than ham licences, which use different frequencies and are heavily regulated. I plotted *Achates*' position and, judging from the course they were steering, I assumed that they were also heading to Tonga, from New Zealand.

After midnight the wind did start to back to the south, as forecast. I rolled along well enough in the abnormally large and increasing swells. I was using the electronic autopilot, as the seas shook the wind out of the sails, making it hard to keep a consistent heading despite Ratso's (the wind vane's) best efforts.

The breeze continued to back enticingly towards the east, like the trades I was expecting. However, it remained light, fickle, and inconsistent. I was working hard for any gains and was routinely called to adjust sails and fiddle with the trim to try and make the best of the conditions and make progress towards my destination of Nuku'alofa, on the island of Tongatapu. Like Raro, it was the southernmost island in its group and the capital, in this case of the Kingdom of Tonga, otherwise known as The Friendly Islands. They were so named by Captain James Cook as he passed through on his second round-the-world voyage in 1773.

Navigationally this leg was quite straightforward, with no real obstructions or reefs to worry about. However, I did pay particular attention to a vigia marked on the chart in a position reported as 'unconfirmed from 1945'. Even though dubiously located, these areas are worth avoiding as you never quite know what may be there, whether a sea mount or something else that can cause confused seas or weird currents. At some point in history, a cautious navigator or watch-keeper has noted something unusual in the vicinity; it makes sense to defer to the Hydrographer of the Navy by giving such places a wide berth.

Although we were making good average speeds each day, the continual large, rolling seas made life difficult. The boat never seemed to get in the groove and often we were kicked off course by a larger than usual wave. It was so rough that I would often have to take the helm or risk an accidental gybe or tack.

Tuning in to the radio net the following night, I again heard *Achates* check in, reporting their position and that they were hove to in 35–40-knot northerly winds. From the position and condition reports of other yachts on the net, it seemed that I was sailing in the best zone for the time being, with winds at around 20 knots. Boats east of the Cook Islands were reporting winds over 30 knots, and boats south of Tonga, coming up from New Zealand, were, like *Achates*, making hard work in heavy weather to get north into the milder, yet elusive, tropics.

Over the next couple of days the winds alternated in direction, and were reliably unreliable. Late on day five a black, incredibly angry-looking squall line blocked the sky to sea level. We were inundated with heavy rain and hammered by strong winds, at first from the north, then switching to blow strongly from the south-west, right on the nose as the front passed. I had pre-emptively triple-reefed the mainsail, but I was forced to dump even that small sail until things settled down and I could get going again.

The fresh headwinds persisted for the remainder of the passage, knocking me no matter which course I took. I was forced to tack and tack, back and forth across our course. It was a continual battle to gain ground.

After nine and a half days I was in sight of the island of Eua in the Tonga group, and I found myself with two options: sail north around the top of the reefs and islets surrounding Tongatapu, then down through the reefs into Nuku'alofa, as had been my original intention; or take the closer, more direct, though perhaps just as challenging, eastern option, via Piha Passage.

The winds had forced me to end up near Eua Island, and I was loath to add more time to the passage by sailing the extra distance back up and through the northern pass. Weighing it up, I felt the risk was similar either way.

I was again without a motor, as cooling system issues continued to plague me. I had been unable to get any decent or recent charts for the area, and was navigat-

A small squall cloud with rain

ing on an old, faded, photocopied chart that lacked detail. There was little specific information on the Piha Passage, only a label indicating a gap through the reef, with a tricky, sharp, 90-degree turn, named The Narrows. I felt it was worth the effort to save about 40 miles. I knew it had been done before, and there was something to be said for getting in for lunch.

Referring to one of Eric Hiscock's books, I found a section describing an occasion when he and Susan had sailed through the same entrance in the 30-foot *Wanderer III* in August 1960:

> *"... swept in through the eastern approach channel where to starboard lay a chain of little windswept motus, with palms so tightly packed there was room for no more, and the outermost leant seaward on all sides. We wriggled through the narrows, and still with plenty of light to see the reefs, made our way across the large and poorly sheltered bay towards the town of Nuku'alofa."*
> — *Beyond the West Horizon*, Eric Hiscock

Scant information indeed, but it did give me confidence to attempt the pass, providing some perspective as I sailed in otherwise blind. I found it just as Eric had described, with overcrowded palms and reefs clearly distinguishable on either side of the five-mile-deep, tapering passage between the reefs, and culminating in a 90-degree turn at The Narrows. These were certainly appropriately named, being only about 0.1 mile wide. I ran in for half a mile or so, gybing at the corners, before the passage opened out into the wider bay. As much as my fluky engine was frustrating, it forced me to make these manoeuvres under sail, which was challenging and always satisfying and appealed to my purist side.

Making my way over the same blustery bay, in the wake of *Wanderer III*, I entered the small breakwater entrance to Faua Harbour, tying alongside a motor boat which was berthed conveniently against the seawall. It was exactly ten days since I had left Rarotonga and the leg had not been without its challenges. It was nice to get in... and it wasn't too late a lunch!

XXVII

Nuku'alofa

Having arrived on a weekend, it was to be a couple of days before I checked in with the friendly customs officers on Tongatapu. Once I had my bearings I moved the boat to another berth, still inside the breakwater, with stern lines led ashore and an anchor out forward among the other yachts in harbour. There were comparatively more Australian and Kiwi boats now, and mixing with this casual group and hearing the familiar accents and vocabulary I'd missed over the previous few years heightened the sense of being closer to home and my anticipation of seeing my family and friends again.

Initially I had hoped to stop for only a few days, collect mail, and have a break before setting off on the final leg – my longest since leaving the Marquesas. However, even though still well in the tropics at 21 degrees south latitude, Tonga comes under the influence of winter low-pressure systems that slide out from mainland Australia. These systems enter the Tasman Sea, making quite an impact over the Western Pacific and often generating strong, persistent, westerly winds where you would hope still to find helpful south-east trade winds.

I had started to come under the influence of these fronts and low-pressure systems even earlier, towards the Cook Islands, and it was testing my patience to be stuck in Nuku'alofa, with heavy winds from the west making it difficult for me to leave.

I bided my time by taking long walks, exploring the town and further afield on the small island. It was roughly triangular in shape, about 24 by 13 kilometres at most. I called by the post office regularly looking for mail. Cindy was good at keeping in touch, sending news of her and Annie, and also a small Tongan courtesy flag that she had made. *Deus Regit II* looked more formal with it flying at the starboard spreaders.

I got to know several of the other visiting sailors in the harbour and several times shared a meal with an Aussie couple, Kim and Carmel, on their trimaran, *Parao*, from near Brisbane. They had two little kids – a boy and a girl – and Kim, a retired police officer, was good for a laugh, always telling stories. The weather was a recurring topic, and we would study print-outs of the synoptic situation from weather faxes that I scrounged from one or other of the commercial ships berthed nearby or from a neighbouring yacht. We combined the fax information with radio reports of conditions from vessels at sea as we watched for a weather window that would see me on my way.

During my time in Nuku'alofa, a group of the Europa Rally boats arrived to rendezvous before starting the next phase of their circumnavigation. I had first seen and admired one of the boats in the Marquesas – the 50-footer *Gilmar Express*, owned by Italian sailor Pasquale De Gregorio. I was pleased to be invited on board one afternoon, and after being shown over the boat I was impressed by the lightweight construction and performance-orientated design.

I was also excited to hear that Pasquale intended to enter the next BOC Challenge, and that he was making plans for a new boat to be built once the Europa Rally had ended. As I told him that I planned to enter the same race, I was struck by the obvious contrast between his fine boat and my small, and by comparison unimpressive, low-tech floating home anchored not far away along the quay. (Pasquale didn't make it to the 1994–95 BOC Challenge, but competed in a later edition of the Vendee Globe solo nonstop round-the-world race).

The Chilean Navy's sail training ship, the barque *Esmeralda*, was also in town, and I got to know a couple of young midshipmen, Christian and Nelson, who were having the time of their lives sailing the classic tall ship around the world with, apart from the regular crew, about 100 other young naval officers in training. We bumped into each other in town and they were fascinated by the freedom I was enjoying and by the fact that I was making long passages on a boat smaller than their ship's lifeboats. We visited each other's vessels – though I was probably more impressed to tour the *Esmeralda* than they were by *Deus Regit II*. I was intrigued to notice, on the bridge, a small, simplified model of the four-masted ship, which was used by the young officers to preview and visualise the sequence of movements required for the myriad of yards and sails before the boat was put about through a gybe or a tack. The midshipmen also enjoyed checking out *Deus Regit II* and were good company during the few visits and meals we shared while in port.

It was now the end of June, and Cindy was due to give birth in only four weeks. I was aware of the need to get moving again if I was going to be home in time for the arrival of the baby. I was set to leave one Friday, but the weather was still too strong from the west, and I was having trouble finding decent forecast information. The Tongan navy patrol boat I had befriended had run out of weather fax paper, and the local radio station had few weather details as the wind's direction didn't seem to much affect life on shore. I was feeling a little frustrated at the delays to my departure.

Eventually, after about ten days, the weather forecasts indicated an imminent break that would finally allow me to leave with a more positive outlook – at least for the first section of the passage. I planned to sail towards New Caledonia, passing to the south of the island and then making more directly towards Newcastle, our home port on the east coast of Australia.

XXVIII

Heading Home:
Gales and More

CASTING OFF THE LINES on Sunday afternoon, I was surprised to discover that the outboard motor was inoperable. It had worked fine the day before! But two mechanics – Pila and Suli – from the Tongan navy patrol boat moored on the other side of the sea wall, along with Kim from *Parao*, helped me to take it apart in the navy ship's workshop to repair the gear lever, which had seized.

It was a relief to be finally on the move again after the weekend. Having spent much longer in Tongatapu than my schedule allowed, I was feeling under the hammer to make a swift passage, and excited about the prospect of getting home to Cindy and Annie, with our new baby about to arrive. However, a small boat has a mind of its own, especially entering new weather regions. A lot can happen in 2000 miles – the distance I had yet to travel – and I knew the weather was likely to be unsettled.

I was taking this passage very seriously; it was to be my longest solo sail to date. Expecting headwinds to be an issue before long, I had cut about 20 metres off the anchor chain, storing it further aft to reduce weight in the bow and hopefully enable me to sail faster and more steadily. I was sure that this small effort would have a measurable effect over the distance.

Once clear of the reefs we made a nice start; the south-easterly had finally returned, even if the trades were a little patchy. The following day I fell into my usual routine of listening to the maritime radio nets each evening. I was surprised to hear Kim from *Parao* on the net to Kerikeri radio in New Zealand, discussing *Deus Regit* and my route to Newcastle. John at Kerikeri agreed to estimate my position based on an average of 100 miles per day, and read out a personalised forecast for me each evening. I was extremely grateful for this initiative – it would be interesting to see for how long my real course and John's estimated one would coincide!

After three days of patchy breeze the weather became overcast, with squally clouds and persistent rain. The wind was flicking about and we were jostled by a big, rolly swell from the south-west.

Kerikeri Radio gave a position for me that was close to my actual, with forecasts of easterlies around 25 knots – still good! My sun sights showed that I was well on track, but the sea grew rough. I saw a ship, *Tasman Asia*, punching south into the swell, and it gave me some perspective regarding the scale of the sea state. The favourable 30-knot wind and torn-up counter swell indicated the influence of another weather system further off.

I was feeling like we were achieving something, being now in the Eastern Hemisphere, having crossed the International Date Line earlier that day, 4 July. (I had been on the Australian date since Tonga. The date line bends around the island group, to retain some regional consistency, though physically the islands are east of 180 degrees, at 175 degrees west.) It was another milestone and a good mark of progress.

The fifth day was heavily overcast, with low, wet clouds. I got no fix that day. During the night, the wind headed us through the west and we started to beat in a moderate south-westerly. Home suddenly seemed far away. Fortunately, the wind backed around after several hours, and easterly winds carried us for a few more days. I was able to use the spinnaker for periods, though generally conditions were unstable and I felt we were on borrowed time.

With our baby due in a few weeks, I felt I was running late. I was apprehensive that I might be held up by contrary winds, and the looming obstacle of typically increasing cold fronts as I headed west made it hard to relax. Forecasts beyond my position showed plenty of these fronts, but so far, thankfully, they were fading or moving off as I approached.

Once again, the daily radio scheds were a useful source of information. I was hearing boats check in that I hadn't seen or heard of for many months. John and Gudrun, sailing from Canada on *Speedwell*, reported their position en route to the Solomon Islands. *Halcyon* was nearing Suwarrow (Suvorov) in the Northern Cooks.

During the day, though I'd never done it much before, I tended to have Radio Australia broadcasting news and world affairs in the background. The familiar sound of the national broadcaster on short wave made me feel closer to home.

Years before, in the North Pacific on our outbound passage up to Canada, Cindy and I had an interesting link with the ABC. The announcer read out a letter from one of the members of the Australian Antarctic Research Expedition, at the time based on Macquarie Island, deep in the Southern Ocean. The letter was from Peter Bourke, who I had grown up with. The Bourkes had kids matching most of my siblings' ages, so we all spent a lot of time together and the families were good friends. I hadn't been in contact with Peter directly since we were children, though I'd known of his exploits and that he was working in Antarctica. That broadcast had put us in touch again, sparking a correspondence from the North Pacific – a nice link from the past for us both, from one remote location to another.

Listening one afternoon to one of the maritime mobile nets, I was gobsmacked to hear that Brunella and Eduardo on the Italian yacht *Lea*, whom I had met when we shared the seawall at Rarotonga, had run solidly up onto Beveridge Reef, a small, low atoll about 350 miles east of Tonga at latitude 20. It was a remote and dangerous situation, but fortunately the crew were safe. My good mate Doug, on *Halcyon*, took the distress call and began handling traffic for emergency response, relaying information via net control to nearby vessels and authorities. There was talk of salvage, but I wasn't able to discover the outcome of the grounding, or if they were refloated. The news of my friends' difficulties was unsettling, to say the least. It's always a little personal when you hear of another vessel in trouble – a reminder that none of us is immune from making a mistake.

Meanwhile, 40-knot winds were forecast for my area and I had my hands full setting up for the heavy weather. I'd reached the half-way mark, averaging a little over 110 miles per day in the up-and-down conditions – overall it was reasonable progress. But my half-way party was a bit flat, as I spiked the stew with too much chilli!

By 11 July the wind was firmly from the west and building; I was close-hauled and *Deus Regit* was bravely chugging away, close to her limits. The heavy winds hit from the north, backing through the west – typical of an approaching cold front. But the winds hung around, reluctant to follow the usual rules: a change through the west would normally be followed by southerlies as the front moved across; however in this instance the low planted itself and blew hard from the west.

My heading was such that I could still lay the course towards Newcastle, but I inadvertently allowed myself to be forced south of my intended route. Even though I was working hard and my small boat was punching valiantly, with three reefs and the storm jib sheeted on tight, we slid sideways.

I'd intended to gradually drop in latitude once past New Caledonia, curving gently in towards the northern New South Wales coast. I should have been sailing well to the north of Middleton and Elizabeth reefs; when clear of these dangers, I could make more directly towards home. However, each day the strong westerlies pushed me closer to the reefs.

When I worked out my position and realised how far, and how fast, I had been pushed south, I thought I might just clear Middleton by about 30 miles to the north – which was safe enough – but it was not to be. The gale increased, and I ended up hove to in winds well above 40 knots. With no hope of progress, let alone of safely clearing the reefs, we hunkered down. I was forced to duck down the back on the leeward side of the reefs, bearing away under small jib alone to avoid being pushed up onto the reefs. Calculating the distance till I would be clear of them, I hoped that within about 18 hours, and once the front had gone through, I might be able to lay over on the other tack and head west, coming out of it not too badly. But this was wishful thinking.

By now, John's nightly estimate of my position broadcast on Kerikeri Radio differed dramatically from the reality – I was several hundred miles further south and significantly further west, so the weather forecasts he so kindly offered each day had no real relevance.

It may seem that all I did was eavesdrop on the radio, but even in the severe gale it was interesting and fun listening to people calmly reporting their position and conditions on the evening schedule. I had heard the well-known Australian solo sailor Jon Sanders checking in as he left New Zealand that week on a non-stop passage over the top of Australia to his home port in Freemantle, Western Australia. He was on the last leg of his seventh circumnavigation. (As I write, Jon is part way through his tenth voyage around the world.) A nonstop passage of over 5000 miles seemed like a walk in the park for him.

Apart from my solo sailing aspirations, Jon and I had one thing in common that week – we shared the same gales! I heard him casually describing to John at Kerikeri radio the heavy seas and more than 40-knot winds that he was dealing with in his 39-foot *Perie Banou II*. For me it was an opportunity to learn from a master with vast experience and literally years at sea, so I listened avidly when I could.

One day we were thrashing away in the dark to windward, not going any-where, and it felt like the boat was a mess. Water was leaking into the forward cabin, from a crack in the drain for the anchor well which had opened up again, and my bunk was soaked. I felt I was doing the right thing, carrying sail and thrashing poor *Deus Regit II* headlong into crashing seas, heeled over on her ear. It was almost impossible for me to do anything but hold on as I listened to reports of boats in various regions around us, most to the east, having an easier time than me. Jon came on the radio, reporting to Kerikeri without apparent concern the rough weather conditions in his region. He was further north but at a similar longitude to me, and in the grip of the same large area of low pressure and strong gale-force conditions. He described his afternoon hove to, reading and relaxing, and how he had been baking and was enjoying some hot scones straight out of the oven and dripping with jam, and a nice cup of tea. This was in stark contrast to my experience of not eating at all – it was just too hard!

Later that night I followed his example: I headed *Deus Regit II* into the wind and hove to. We were not making any progress anyway, so I might as well take the pressure off and slow things down in an effort to get some rest and keep the boat in one piece.

The seas were terrible – breaking and confused – and my only option was to keep going until the westerly wind eased or shifted enough to allow me to head west. I didn't want to head north again, merely retracing my steps, as I was still expecting the wind to swing into the south, and eventually back to the trades. But it didn't, continuing to blow westerly gales for several more days.

I usually kept the cabin companionway open to let in air and light, even if it was a bit tough outside. However, being smashed and thrown about in these forceful seas I ended up not only dropping in the top washboard, effectively closing the door, but I also got out the tools and screwed a barrel bolt to the top segment, locking the boards firmly in place so they could not move or jump out of position as the heavy seas poured over us. How does that song go? "Stop the world, I want to get off!"

Although the weather remained mostly sunny, it was extremely difficult when taking sun sights to find a real horizon among the waves. Still, with some effort I was able to fix my position most days. The solar panel was keeping the batteries amply charged, allowing me to show a masthead light at night.

Nothing changed once I passed the reefs – I was still only able to make a southerly heading. Lord Howe Island was the next obstruction and it was déjà vu as I couldn't head up any closer to the wind to get past, and risked being pushed down onto the island. For a while I entertained the idea of anchoring behind Ned's Beach, on the north-eastern side of the island, to try to contact Cindy, to see if she had had the baby and to let her know where I was. But in the conditions, I had no chance of making it cleverly into the anchorage, let alone putting down enough rode to hold me safely in that open roadstead.

I was forced to sail south around the island, rather than over the top, as I would have preferred. For four days I laboured down the back of the reefs, and then the island, alternately sailing and being hove to. Sailing was preferable, as it was mind numbing to stop and wait. By this stage I'd forgotten *Perie Banou*'s example of being patient and relaxing when there was nothing else you could do!

When the sun came up on day 16 I could see Ball's Pyramid, a great shard of rock more than 500 metres high, piercing the sky like the fin of a giant shark. It lies about 15 miles south and a bit east of Lord Howe, and I was able to take a bearing, which I crossed with a sun line for a rough fix.

Battening down the hatches, I remained hove to until the next morning. Then, as the wind swung around with some south in it, I put the boat about and was able to head vaguely north-west, and start to make some progress again. I still

Tasman Sea gales – a nice day out, except it occasionally blew 40kts (for days)...

had to defer to Lord Howe and retrace my recent traverse down the east side, as it would have been impossible for me to claw past to windward of the island in those conditions.

Even in the lee of Lord Howe the gale was blowing 40 knots or more, pushing us sideways. The sea was still high and very rough, and I was hard-pressed not to lose ground. However, by 20 July we were finally on the Australian side – near where I might have been early on the 16th! Overall, in six days we had made good only 180 miles towards home. At one point, as the breaking top of a big wave churned and hit us, the boat spun horizontally through 360 degrees like a top! It was awesome – something I've never experienced before or since.

I know that difficult days are quickly forgotten once settled weather sets in or a safe haven is reached. But in the midst of it I was run ragged, snacking occasionally on a sticky spoonful of jam to boost my energy. It was a full-time job tending to the boat, with little rest or sleep. I took great encouragement from the seabirds flitting about in their natural element, seemingly unfazed.

I felt impatient; I wanted to be in port and get news of Cindy and the kids. I feared she might have already had the baby without me there for support. Of course, at home in Newcastle she was busy with her own stuff, not too worried about me nor the timing. I always admire Cindy's innate ability to remain calm about things out of her control. But for me, at sea and feeling rundown, it was harder to be pragmatic.

Before I left Tonga, I had heard from home that one of the Newcastle newspapers had run a small article about the fact that Cindy and I were sailing back to Australia. This was a kind of follow up to a front-page story and picture of us on the boat published by the same paper before we set off across the Pacific on our honeymoon in 1987. It had caused a stir at the time, and for some reason people remembered and there was some public interest in hearing about our adventures over the succeeding years. The piece ended with the revelation that I was planning to enter the BOC race, which was coming up in a few years. I don't even remember how this story got out there – perhaps a call to family for comment – but it was an interesting detail that later helped springboard our campaign to enter the round-the-world race.

The winds teased me, abating briefly, only to return with a vengeance as another cold front swept into the Tasman, bringing drenching rain and rough, unruly seas. Hove to around midnight, I imagined – if she were with me – turning downwind and escaping to Queensland with Cindy.

The possibility of making it home any time soon evaporated. Not relishing the prospect of continuing to struggle dead upwind in gales, I abandoned the plan to sail to Newcastle, deciding instead to head for Coffs Harbour, about 150 miles north-west – a much more achievable goal. Importantly, Coffs was familiar; it was also a customs port where I could officially enter, so a good option – the only option really.

Overnight on 23 July conditions eased, though the wind was twitching and gusting in speed and direction, and I thought I may not even make Coffs Harbour. I was tired and I imagined the boat felt tired, though *Deus Regit II* had been brilliant, slogging away in conditions that would be hard for much larger vessels. But she was reliable and solid, apart from a few minor leaks.

Early in the morning I caught sight of land for the first time since glimpsing Lord Howe, nearly five days earlier. It turned out to be ranges lying inland from the coast, and was much further away than it looked. As the breeze tapered off, it became a lovely sunny day, with brilliant blue sky and unhindered visibility, typical of the Australian winter. Whales were blowing nearby.

By noon I was drifting, and I calculated I was 35 miles east of Coffs. I was light on fuel and hesitant to start up the outboard too soon. Later, I spoke to a car-carrier ship en route to Port Villa in Vanuatu, and they placed me about 5 miles closer than my calculations suggested. Thinking I might just make it with the 10 litres I had on board, I kicked the 6-horsepower motor into life and started chugging away. It felt perversely satisfying to be going in a straight line for a change.

Even in the calmer winds, a big greasy swell remained, the legacy of the recent heavy weather and the previous three lows and fronts. I was able to shut the engine down for a couple of hours to save fuel, but I was keen to get in, so as soon as the breeze eased further, the motor went on without any guilt.

Typically, as night falls on the coast, the cooler, denser air rolls off the land over the sea, creating an offshore breeze. Soon it was blowing 20 knots from the west, exactly from where I was heading. I was jaded, having to respond with some effort and actually sail in after such a mellow afternoon.

Though I advised Coffs coastal patrol on VHF of my pending arrival, no one thought to mention that the gales and big seas had closed out the harbour entrance with breaking waves all week. I hadn't factored in the leftover groundswell, until *Deus Regit II*, between the breakwater and a small island that forms the harbour mouth, was suddenly lifted high. She went sliding down the face of a 3-metre breaking crest and was spat out into the choppy, but comparatively smoother, water within.

At 9:30 p.m., after 23 days and 10 hours at sea, I put down an anchor near the old jetty in the outer harbour. The jetty was an ancient thing where steamers used to load, and in the 1950s my grandfather and other local fishermen had lifted their trawlers out here with a crane, cradling them for maintenance or when bad weather ripped up the coast. Thankful and weary, I asked the duty officer at coastal patrol to phone Cindy and let her know that I had arrived. I would clear customs in the morning.

XXIX

Coastal Hop: Easy!

WITH CUSTOMS FORMALITIES completed, I was finally able get off the boat and speak with Cindy. It was good to hear that the baby was still firmly situated and apparently in no rush to join the rest of humanity on the outside. With the pressure off, I had a day and a half in port tidying up, giving the sea and wind time to settle down. The final couple of hundred miles to Newcastle to close our Pacific circuit should be an easy leg.

Typically, when passage-making on a coast, it's all about timing. I set off in the evening, to make it as far as I could before the next cold front. It was a slog sailing into headwinds, but at least I was on my way and could count on the wind lifting as the existing system progressed. The following day was nice sailing: the wind was with me and fairly light; the lumpy chop had flattened out and I was averaging about five knots over the ground, sometimes motor-sailing to keep up a consistent pace.

Being back in Australia was satisfying, and I was in a better frame of mind knowing Cindy was well, and that I hadn't missed the delivery. I was enjoying seeing the colours of the Australian bush again: from the sea, the coast looks dark, its heavy greens and greys backlit by the sun, with gold and orange merging into the deep blue evening sky. Combined with the bold headlands and other familiar features of the coast, it was a visual feast and a contrast to the (equally impressive) open horizon that had been my view for weeks. It all seemed new after several years away. Appealing locations that would offer convenient stopovers had I been cruising without time constraints slipped by, and I hoped that one day I would be able to explore the area slowly with Cindy and the children.

Sugarloaf Point, about 60 miles north-east of Newcastle, is a significant headland I have learnt to treat with respect. It is a major turning point where the coast bends to run in a south-west/north-east direction. The headland seems be a magnet for cold fronts, sucking them into that significant hook of land as they roll up the coast, before bouncing out into the Tasman Sea. This creates local conditions, sometimes delineating a different weather region from one side to the other. The funnelling effect often produces higher speed winds than forecast, and if your passage coincides with a south-westerly change you can count on a difficult rounding and slog out the other side.

With this awareness of its reputation, I felt as though I was getting away with something when I sailed past Sugarloaf before dawn in still water and light winds. I was on the home straight with about 50 miles to go – one more headland and a hop across Stockton bight would see me in by nightfall.

However, my final run home wasn't to be so easy. The early morning Sydney radio forecast reported that a front was belting up the New South Wales coast; strong to gale-force winds were expected in the evening on the Hunter Coast off Newcastle. If the timing of the forecast was accurate, I had about 12 hours; I might be cutting it fine if the front was earlier than predicted, which is often the case.

At the halfway mark – Point Stephens, another lesser headland – the forecast gave me about four hours, and the milky sky to the south heralded the imminent change. I anticipated plenty of action. Intuitively, I knew the front was ahead of schedule, as I ventured into Stockton bight for the final 20 miles. The wind was still deceptively favourable, at that point blowing quite hard from the north; but minutes after I heard the latest forecast, it backed suddenly, slamming into us from the south-west and more than doubling in strength. The boat, overwhelmed, was heeled hard over, rounding up into the wind and laying on her side with the windows awash as I hastily tied the second and third reefs into the main and started to furl the genoa.

My goal was almost in sight, but the significant chop whipped up by the onslaught soon brought me to a standstill. I persevered for a couple of hours but was unable to make progress, and was forced to turn around and head back up the coast. It took all day to backtrack only about 12 miles. After initially scooting off fast downwind in that gale until near the entrance, *Deus Regit II* put her game face on as we slogged our way into Port Stephens just before dusk, working tack for tack up the narrow inlet, with shoals on each side, and berthed at the marina in Nelson Bay. I had earlier called the coastguard and relayed a message to Cindy that I would put in for the night, suggesting that she drive up and join me for the weekend.

Cindy was happy to make the hour-long drive up in the small Ford she had bought not long after arriving home. It was wonderful to be reunited with my family – to see Cindy's smile and her healthy bulging tummy, and Annie, grown taller, holding her mum's hand and shyly waving on the dock as I popped into the shelter of the breakwater, bringing *Deus Regit II* alongside. It seemed a very long time since I had last seen them in the Marquesas, but suddenly the passage in between didn't seem so hard.

We found a small, dingy motel near the marina – unfortunately not a very salubrious place to spend our first night on land together in a couple of years. It might have been nicer on board, but the bunks were soaked and it may have been a little musty there too.

The following morning a television crew from the local station, NBN, came to film an interview and talk about our trip. The journalist, Andy Lobb, whom we later came to know well, was a sailor. He was excited about what we had been doing, but quickly jumped forward to discuss the BOC, which was a little off topic for us at that point. However, he ran with that story, announcing that we wouldn't be around long as we were building a boat to race around the world in three years' time. We were thrown in at the deep end – our BOC campaign was officially launched, like it or not! That became everyone's expectation – although at the time we were more focused on establishing a normal life for our little family back on terra firma, trying to keep things simple and mundane for a while.

With the strong wind still blowing, we drove to Cindy's family home at Lake Macquarie. A couple of days later I returned to the boat and completed the final short day sail of 30 or so miles into Newcastle Harbour, then on to Lake Macquarie, wrapping up our wonderful adventure on 31 July – Cindy's official due date!

Epilogue

I T WAS AN IMMENSELY SATISFYING accomplishment for Cindy and me to
have safely completed the journey aboard *Deus Regit II*, with almost 25,000
miles under the keel. Our little crew had grown significantly since we started, and
soon after my arrival we were more than delighted when our son, Vance Eric, was
born. (He was not in a hurry to join us, so a couple of weeks after my return
Cindy's labour had to be induced.) I was able to find a job straight away, and we
rented an apartment that would suit the growing family for the next phase, which
we quickly fell into.

Cindy and I had set out more than four years previously with only a loose
plan: we weren't sure how far we would travel or how long we would be away. I
was fortunate that my passion to sail offshore – originally solo – gave me oppor-

Back in Newcastle – the family aboard Deus Regit II *after Vance's first small cruise on Lake Macquarie* — PHOTO: HILARY HENLEY

tunities to pursue my goals. To have Cindy jump on board to share that journey and lifestyle, with all the associated benefits of a budding relationship, enriched the whole experience immeasurably. She came to love the travel and adventure, seeing new lands and meeting new people; the lifestyle suited her too.

Given that our plans had changed, with the plan to take on the BOC Challenge and with Vance on the way, it had been logical to head back to Australia to start a new chapter and to see if the idea of racing around the world was feasible. Formulating a personal goal from concept, presenting it to the public, and securing endorsement and support was an ambitious initiative and a significant challenge – probably tougher than any passage making in a small yacht! But it did open up an exciting and enjoyable new world.

Just shy of three years later I was back in Newcastle harbour with a new boat – a state-of-the-art 50-footer that was about as different as you could get from the dependable little classic, *Deus Regit II*. Though still a simple boat – brand new, water-ballasted, stripped out and bare, with no engine – the yacht, *Newcastle Australia*, was by comparison loaded with mod cons: satellite communications to receive weather data; a radical new thing called email; single sideband radio; GPS units; and hydraulic and electronic autopilots. It was a different era, and I was fortunate to have been able to bridge the old and new generations of sailing and navigating. The fundamental principles still hold true, but the accuracy and level of sophistication was moving forward in leaps and bounds; we were using pioneering new equipment that has impacted how boats are sailed today, making voyaging safer and faster.

I had inadvertently wedged myself into a tight deadline yet again: I was about to embark on an 11,500-mile shakedown voyage just to get to the start of the 1994–95 BOC Challenge, due to begin in a little over 10 weeks' time on the East Coast of the United States.

That is the beginning of another story – one full of personal and business challenges, enhanced, like most things in life, by the people we met. We made friends and garnered support from the community and corporations. We even met with resistance! There were financial and practical challenges associated with taking on a radical new idea while raising two small children; however, we had a vision and we stuck with it, finding confidence and contentment by following our unique path. In both the simple and the complicated phases, the fact that we have a Christian faith provides us with no small measure of assurance.

Newcastle Australia – *the yacht I would race around the world single-handed in the BOC Challenge race. The story of that adventure is told in my book,* Against All Odds.

PHOTO: STEVE NEBAUER, A BEAR IMAGE

He stilled the storm to a whisper;
the waves of the sea were hushed.
They were glad when it grew calm,
and he guided them to their desired haven.

— Psalm 107:29–30 (New International Version)

Against All Odds

by Alan Nebauer

Against All Odds is the true story of Alan Nebauer's remarkable experiences in the 1994–95 BOC Around the World Race for single-handed sailors. Sailing as a Class II competitor aboard the 50-foot (15.2 m) *Newcastle Australia*, Alan Nebauer had to endure incredible difficulties in a race that lasted almost eight months and covered 27,000 nautical miles.

This book recounts the author's rescue of a fellow English competitor, his experiences of being dismasted and rounding Cape Horn with a jury rig, and the loss of his rudder north of the Falkland Islands, sailing with a steering oar to Uruguay. Beyond this, it is a testament to Alan's extraordinary courage and determination in the face of overwhelming odds, and to his outstanding seamanship for which he deservedly won two awards.

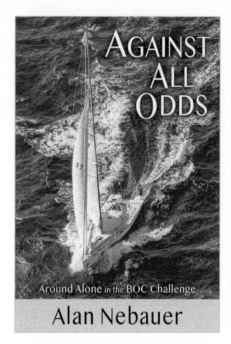

IMPERATOR

2nd edition, 2019

ISBN 978-1-912784-00-4

www.imperator.pub/against-all-odds

Sailing around Cape Horn under jury rig is like climbing Mount Everest in thongs. Alan's seamanship and tenacity is tremendous.

— David Adams

Winner of Class II of the 1994–95 BOC Challenge and competitor in 1990–91

1995 Australian Yachtsman of the Year

Alan Nebauer's love of the sea and his determination not to be defeated by the challenges he faced in the world's most gruelling yacht race is positively contagious. The result is a page-turning thriller that those with an ounce of salt in their veins cannot afford to miss.

— Alan Lucas

Circumnavigator and author

A Family Outing in the Atlantic

by Jill Dickin Schinas

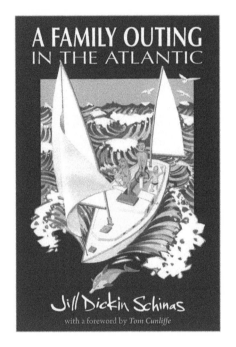

IMPERATOR

2nd edition, 2013

ISBN 978-0-9560722-3-8

www.imperator.pub/family-outing-atlantic

The overriding feature of their lives and the guiding spirit of this book is their self-sufficiency and courage to make their own choices, come fair weather or foul ... Keeping going, despite producing three fine children and surviving a capsize off the Falklands that ended on the winch cable of an RAF helicopter, shows the true spirit of seafaring.

— Tom Cunliffe

British yachtsman and author

" Yes, we were bound for Cape Horn – or at any rate, Patagonia. In as much as we had a destination, this indeed was it. But we were in no great hurry, and even this goal was viewed as little more than a staging post on our journey, for we meant to journey indefinitely. Truly, it was not a place but a lifestyle which we were setting forth to find."

On the face of it, this book is a travelogue telling the story of a seven-year long cruise which ended on the winch cable of an RAF chopper. Before arriving at this premature end the family had already wandered far from the path followed by most yachtsmen, blazing a trail which had led them to explore such places as Guinea Bissau, Ghana, the Amazon, and Ilha Trindade; thus, the story is unique in the annals of sailing lore. Still, this is but half the value of the book, for woven between the tale of their adventures is a portrait of the cruising lifestyle.

There is much here that will be of interest to other yachtsmen and other travellers, and heaps which will appeal to other families seeking to turn away from the nine-to-five motorway and tread a road of their own.

Lightning Source UK Ltd.
Milton Keynes UK
UKHW010917200919
350146UK00003B/523/P